No Mean Feat

the autobiography of

Ann Gillanders

ISBN 0 9511868 1 7

Prepared for publication by
Jenny Lee Publishing Services
Bishop's Stortford, Herts.
Phototypeset by
Hart-Talbot Printers Limited
Saffron Walden, Essex.
Printed in Great Britain by
J. W. Arrowsmith Ltd
Bristol

Dedicated to my children
Mark, Clare, Jonathan and Heather

For information about Reflexology
write to:

The British School of Reflexology
Holistic Healing Centre,
92 Sheering Road,
Old Harlow,
Essex, CM17 0JT
Tel. 0279 29060

Contents

Introduction

It is 40 years now since I was stricken with polio and this event totally changed the direction of the pathway of the life I was intended to follow.

It is 22 years since John died and my children are now grown up, but so much has happened to us all in the intervening years that I feel bound to bring my story up to date, not now for the sake of my children, but for the benefit of my little grandson James and any future grandchildren. For them this will be a little bit of their own history which, in later years, when they are able to read and understand for themselves, may seem even more remarkable to them than it does to me or to their parents.

Life has treated me kindly on the whole, and I have succeeded in riding its storms which have been many and varied. Nothing that has happened to me has made me change my mind about the things in life that count the most. I am still the same person with the same ideals, but with greater experiences than I could ever have dreamt possible.

I hope that by relating these events I may be able to help others to climb their own particular ladder and surmount their own individual problems, things that are the common heritage of us all, whoever and wherever we may be.

This was never intended to be more than an ordinary love story, not just the love of man and woman, or mother and child, but true love of my fellow-men. I am not extraordinary but human and fallible. The only difference is that I have a considerable disability, and my life's aim has been to prove that a disability is of little consequence when set against the reality of being a person with a character and a mind as unique as any other.

Self-realisation is the key

After a while you learn the subtle difference between holding a hand or chaining a soul – and you learn that love does not mean security, kisses are not contracts and presents are not promises. You also begin to accept defeats with your head up and your eyes open – with the grace of a woman, not the grief of a child.

And after a while you learn to build all your own roads on today because tomorrow's ground is too uncertain and futures have a way of collapsing in midflight, and even sunshine burns if you get too much. So you plan your own garden and decorate your own soul – instead of waiting for someone to bring *you* flowers.

And after a while you learn to find your God.

A.G.

1 Childhood memories

I was born in March 1940, shortly after the outbreak of the Second World War. During the actual war years we lived with my grandparents, Gran and Grandad (always called Harry), my mother's sister, Kitty, and my Aunt Rose. We lived in one of those large terraced houses in North London, with lots of rooms and all sorts of nooks and crannies everywhere. I cannot recall much about the war years (which is just as well), apart from the night when I left my much-loved doll behind in the bedroom during an air raid and there was a tremendous scrabble to find this doll and bring it to me in the shelter where we all huddled.

My close family consisted of my father, a rather nervous man of average build, with thick fair curly hair, very fair complexion and blue eyes. My mother, on the other hand, was really beautiful with a head of the darkest, most luxuriant hair, dark eyes and an olive skin. During the summer months she tanned so naturally that many people thought she was of Italian descent. She had a very gentle nature, was loved by everyone, and hardly ever became cross.

Gran was a very gracious lady, a tower of strength who had supported Harry, her weak alcoholic husband, for years. She had successfully run businesses all her life in order to be both mother and father to her three children, Kitty, Betty (my mother) and George, the youngest. First she was a very fine dressmaker, and later ran a successful pub called 'The Rose and Crown' in Highgate Village, North London, where she cooked traditional roast lunches for the local gentry and fought proudly to send her children to good schools. The children were always well turned-out, in good-quality clothes which Gran made from well-trimmed market remnants, and the Traceys, which was the family name, were a well-respected family considered to be a cut above average.

Eventually the pub had to be sold as Harry drank away all the profits. In his drunken stupors he would lend large sums of money to any local customer who claimed to have fallen upon hard times, and then could never remember to whom he had given the loan. He had obviously been a passenger whom Gran had pitied and protected all her married life, but eventually he was loathed not only by her but by the children as well.

I shall always remember Gran, and in some ways I feel we shared great similarities of character. She was so refined and elegant in her attractive home-made silk dresses trimmed with a lace ruff at the neck, all made from 'good buys' at the local drapers and lovingly put together on her ancient sewing machine. Her fine grey hair was well looked after, and she always smelt of lavender which was her only luxury. A large bottle of lavender water was usually given to her on her birthday and at Christmas by some member of the family. As she opened the drawers where she kept her personal linen, there, neatly arranged between the whiter than white sheets, were small cushions of dried lavender. Whenever I smell lavender in the garden today it always reminds me of Gran.

Her cooking was superb, she baked cakes and made jars and jars of jams, chutneys, mincemeat and pickles to last throughout the year.

During her later years she kept very much to routine. She suffered unfortunately from bouts of nervous indigestion, no doubt caused by the years of hard work and responsibility, plus the worry of Harry's drinking, and her desperate efforts to maintain certain standards in her life which were so important to her. To ease her stomach she used to rest after lunch in the 'best room', and I can see her now sitting in a high-backed floral armchair reading the good books which she so much enjoyed, and sucking clear mints which she kept in a tin on the mantlepiece. Next to this tin was a heavy oak-framed clock with attractive carvings. The numerals on this clock were brass and seemed enormous to me as a small child. The relentless and loud ticking of this old clock seemed to resemble Gran, strong, reliable and rather special. My mother has this clock today on her sideboard and so, in a way, Gran chimes on.

I used to sit with Gran in the 'best room', which was really a very private place, used only for her afternoon rest, entertaining and high days and special days, and she often spoke to me about the days in the Rose and Crown, her 'Highgate days', the days when we had money and security. She worked in that pub for about eleven years, building up what was a very run-down business into a high-class restaurant, frequented by all the local solicitors, doctors and businessmen, and she became highly respected for her excellent traditional English cooking.

Everything changes, even the bad things, so they say, and Gran's 'good life' came to an end when, because of Harry's constant drinking, they decided to move out to a smallholding in Essex. Harry really was 'green-fingered' – that was about the only thing he could do well – and Gran hoped that if he were occupied with growing things and far away from the pubs, his problem might improve. It did, and he did well with 'growing things', but financially the smallholding became a disaster and the family lost all their money.

Gran went on with Harry until the end of his days, feeding and caring for him just as if he were a little child who never grew up. I am sure she must have suffered agonies of frustration and longed for a true soulmate, as she was such a fine, handsome, capable woman and certainly worthy of far more, but in those days couples used to stick together 'until death do us part'.

I suppose most families adopt from each other habits or standards that go on year after year and in some cases generation after generation, and ours was no exception. These habits somehow become almost 'engraved on your soul'. Simple things like the way my mother peeled and cored apples, peeled potatoes, sliced runner beans, I do in exactly the same way, but in our family there were far more important things. Above all, great emphasis was placed on diction. Gran and my mother constantly checked me and later my cousins for dropping an 'h' or not sounding the ends of our words, and generally the use of both spoken or written English was considered of paramount importance in our general development. My mother was excellent at writing and her use of the English language was near perfect. We were encouraged to read the classics when it came to choosing books. Table manners, tidiness, learning to respect other people's possessions, the way you dressed were all important. Gran would not even go out to buy a loaf of bread without being properly dressed, wearing a hat, gloves, and well-polished shoes and always with a nice brooch on her overcoat. These standards were nothing to do with money, as none of us had any – it was just our attempt to nurture the social niceties or graces of life.

I found all this a terrible bore as a child, but as I have become older I have realised that these standards are 'very special' in my life too, and anything crude, coarse or brash is abhorrent to me. I always remember Gran saying, 'There are many people who master several languages to perfection; it surely cannot be much of an effort to speak just one language well.'

I can just remember my Dad returning from the war. He arrived in uniform one day with a kitbag brim-full of goodies. He emptied the contents into a heap in the middle of our living room. There were presents for all – a plaid skirt on a bodice for me with a very fine pair of leather shoes, plus a large tin of peanut butter and an equally enormous tin of corned beef.

My brother Tony was born at the end of the war, in 1945. I really cannot remember too much about him as a baby, except that, just like Dad, he had a mass of tight curls, which stayed with him for years, and enormous blue eyes. He was a very sensitive, emotionally fragile little boy, who was always good and almost angelic in expression. I was much more of a rebel, outgoing and with a mind and will of my own. I joined all the usual things that little girls do – Brownies, a tap-dancing class – and had lots of friends. During the school holidays, we used to spend nearly the whole day in our local woods, climbing trees, wading through streams and getting soaked to the skin, collecting wild flowers, acorns, berries. With a bottle of lemonade and a packet of sandwiches we made our own fun.

I always fancied myself as a nurse. I used to make wards on my bedroom floor and line up my dolls in all sorts of prone positions. With splints for their limbs made from lollipop sticks, bandages for their 'wounds', I was well away – Florence Nightingale the second. My adored Persian cat Twinkle was so docile that he was quite happy to be dressed in a gown and laid in a cot, so he became another of my 'patients'.

In 1947 we moved into our own home only a couple of miles away from Gran. It was a semi-detached house on three levels. We had the ground and first floors and the top was let off as a separate flat to sitting tenants. We really felt quite special owning a house of our own. There was a large garden where my mother kept chickens and grew vegetables.

My mother hand-reared chicks around an old tilley lamp. It was sheer magic waiting for the first crack to appear on the shell and then a rather bedraggled little chick emerge – within just a few hours the wet bedraggled mass of feathers became a powder puff of golden down. I think children today miss out so much of 'natural pleasure'. I later kept rabbits and hamsters as I was crazy about animals and would have been in heaven with an animal sanctuary. The tears and suffering I went through when my rabbits died and hamsters became ill! I suffered agonies of loss and held frequent funerals in the garden. We had a pet chicken called Blondie, a very large cream Leghorn. Dad fattened her up for Christmas dinner, but when she was brought to the table my brother and I cried and refused to eat any. I kept her wishbone tied up with pink ribbon in a matchbox for years.

Dad worked hard in the garden at weekends and my mother did lots of work outside during the week, how I shall never know, as she also did various part-time jobs. However, everything seemed to fit in.

There was only a tiny scullery in this house, which had absolutely no conveniences or comforts, apart from a butler sink with a cold tap, an ancient gas cooker and two large cupboards, one housing the groceries and china and the other our large supply of coal, the dust from which frequently invaded the scullery floor. However, in this tiny area my mother cooked the most superb meals, baked cakes, apple pies and scones. We never had ready-prepared food in our household.

It is strange how certain routines in childhood become imprinted on your mind. Our weekly shopping trip to our local grocer's was a special occasion, so different from today's visit to the local supermarket, when you walk through spotless aisles with a trolley full to brimming over, faced with a selection of foods that must run into thousands. Eventually you reach the check-out, there to stand in a queue, quite certain in your mind that you have bought enough to feed the family for a couple of weeks, only to find that you have to return the next week for a repeat performance.

Our grocery store was called Dakins. It was a very small shop with a wooden floor and a small range of shelves behind the counter. As soon as my mother and I went in I would be placed on a high polished chair, just high enough for me to be level with the counter. My mother would get out a small blue book – her shopping book – and would religiously tick off every item on her list and record its price. The grocer, always dressed in a white coat, would cut the butter from a large slab and then, with a special cutter, make an impint of an acorn or clover leaf, then wrap it up in white paper. The cheese too was cut from a large block and weighed to your choice. Sugar, tea, coffee and dried fruits were served with scoops from large vats which had glass lids and stood in rows beneath the counter. The scoops were shiny and I am sure were brass. All dry goods were then packed in very tough, dark blue bags, and neatly folded on top. There was no hurry or pressure and we were always treated with the utmost courtesy. The grocer would even pack your shopping bag.

The hardware shop also held special memories. I can still recall the smell of polish, candles and paraffin. We used to buy a special metal cleaning powder which was mixed into a paste and used to clean silver. This had a very pungent smell, but I can't remember what it reminded me of.

My mother used to make most of our clothes on the most dreadful old sewing machine which caused her endless frustration when it cockled up the fabric and was generally more trouble than it was worth. Why she did not down tools and demand a new one I shall never know.

Everything seemed ancient in that house. There was an old boiler in our living room which had a temperament of its own. Sometimes it would heat the water and sometimes it would not, and if the wind was in a certain direction it went out two or three times a day and then all the old coke would have to be raked out, new wood and paper laid inside and another attempt made at persuading it to light and stay alight.

When mother washed on Mondays it was all done by hand, apart from using a large galvanised bucket for boiling. It was always all done in a few hours. However, people did not change their clothes as frequently as they do today.

Sundays were different. Sundays were days of 'special smells', roasting meat, baking: very often the smell of a fruit cake would waft upstairs before I was even up. My father would clean out the chicken pens and there would be an excessive amount of 'clucking' as the hens were disturbed from their usual environment.

Dad worked in London as a very good gentlemen's hairdresser. He used to attend to the hair of film stars or stage actors, and sometimes we would be given complimentary tickets for a show at the Palladium and at Christmas we always had super presents sent to us by his clients.

Another special treat which we occasionally enjoyed was a shopping trip to another local town. At the end of the morning's shopping we would go into Lyons' Corner House and have a buttered bun and a lemonade. My brother and I would feel like the King and Queen. Our pleasures were small ones, we made our own fun without the support of television and all the packaged pleasures of today, yet I am sure we were much happier than today's children who generally find it difficult to create their own entertainment.

My parents, and in fact my entire family, were hard-working and industrious, and that too goes back generations. I was brought up to accept that life was meant to be spent working hard and that very little pleasure should be expected. Unless one ended the day in a state of complete exhaustion something was wrong. This 'guilt complex' for expecting anything else apart from work is still deeply implanted within me today and I am sure that I would be classed as a 'workaholic' in most people's eyes. I have frequently had to condition myself to balance work against leisure. However, I now manage to enjoy far more leisure than ever before, but this has been achieved only in recent years. I am sure that the most successful are those who enjoy their work yet get a lot of fun out of recreation too – not those who feel guilty if they enjoy their leisure.

I went to school at a convent. It had sparsely furnished classrooms with polished wooden floor boards, and the oldest desks you ever saw, so gnarled and pitted that there was hardly an area on the desk flap flat enough to write on. All the equipment we were allowed were white china inkwells that fitted into a hole in the top right-hand corner of the desk, blotting paper and a cracked or broken ruler. The inkwell was the best: if you rolled up bits of blotting paper and dropped them into the ink, they made good pellets to fire at the boys across the class. However, if the nuns caught you, you faced a punishment worse than death, so this pastime was indulged in only rarely.

We seemed to have certain very rigid routines to comply with. One routine in particular is very vivid in my mind, 'polishing' on Friday afternoons, just before we finished for the weekend: a most enormous tin of red wax polish was brought into the class with a pile of clean rags and each pupil then polished every area of her desk, including the legs until you could see your face in it. The prefect for the term then mixed some black powder with a small amount of water and there was our supply of dark blue ink for the following week. Then, with great care, each inkwell was filled.

The nuns were formidable, and I was terrified of most of them. We had to trail behind them carrying their books, total silence was insisted upon as we walked through the corridors, and there was very little freedom of speech in class or at any other time.

We spent our time on rather tedious pursuits such as manuscript writing, or sewing, always boring things like making aprons and hemming handkerchiefs. I found the whole subject of needlework utterly frustrating and still do; to this day it is a great achievement if I turn up a hem straight.

We wore strict conventional school uniform with a navy velour hat during the winter, and a straw hat with elastic under the chin in summer. Hair had to be tied back – I had two very long thick brown plaits, so that was all right. Hats and blazers had to be worn whatever the temperature, and if you were seen chewing sweets or eating while in school uniform, you would be sent to Reverend Mother and punished, normally by pages and pages of manuscript writing, or tidying out the enormous stationery cupboard. The convent was run by an order of French nuns, so the French language was concentrated upon.

I was no great scholar, spending lots of time day-dreaming out of the window about writing essays, articles and great novels, most of which were going to be best-sellers. Most of my great works remained in my mind, although I did have an affinity for writing and in fact English was the only subject that I ever achieved top marks for. School prizes were either for writing essays or plays for the school. Music was my second love, and I sang at most of the school concerts as I had quite a good soprano voice.

However, when it came to mathematics, I used to be given marks only for 'using the paper and ink'!

There was a Hall of Reverence at the Convent in the very oldest part of the school building. Several new extensions had been added over the years to enlarge the school, but there were still only 400 pupils in all. To get to the Hall of Reverence you walked through a beautiful garden with old-established shrubs, dozens of rose trees and a lovely old brick wall which surrounded the whole area. Reverend Mother had her office in the hall, which was thickly carpeted in crimson. A life-sized statue of the Virgin Mary stood in the corner, clad in blue and holding in her hands the crown of thorns. There was always a circle of lighted candles at her feet and small vases of flowers dotted here and there. I used to gaze at this figure and experience a mixture of emotions from awe to fear and trepidation, and vow once again to make greater efforts with my mathematics.

We used the hall every day for a month for prayers when one of the pupils in my class became ill. Pearl was a good friend of mine. She was only eight when a severe blood disease was diagnosed. I rather think now that it was leukaemia, for within a few short weeks she withered away and died.

I had felt sure that praying in the Hall of Reverence every day would save her, and was shattered when she died. I really believed that if you prayed to the Virgin Mary miracles would happen, so my faith in God was much reduced. I remember her funeral as if it were yesterday. All the pupils and staff attended, I gazed at the wreaths and the beautiful decorations in the church and felt the intensity of the mass, then saw that small white coffin on the top of which was a large wreath in the shape of a cross.

I also remember the distress of her parents and the prayers that were offered up for her sins to be forgiven. I found that hard to accept. What sins had Pearl committed at the age of eight that had to be forgiven, and why did good people have to die especially when they were so young? Maybe it was not wearing her hat or perhaps it was flicking pellets across the class? The nuns always said that we would have to ask for forgiveness for these sins. Perhaps that was what the priest meant. Did God make you die young if you committed sins? In any case Pearl was a Catholic, and the nuns always made you feel that Catholics were 'special'.

Most years we managed two weeks away on holiday in either Devon or Cornwall. We usually went with my Auntie Kitty, Uncle Stanley and my two cousins Jean and Keith, and we always stayed in a nice boarding house near the sea.

Although a true Piscean by nature I had a love/hate relationship with the sea. I longed to be able to swim but when it came to actually taking my feet off the bottom I never quite had the confidence. However, in the summer of 1949 on our holiday in Bude, Cornwall, I learned at last to swim, and from that day on the water and I became truly united. At the end of that fortnight I was swimming in the sea with confidence and ease, enjoying being thrown about by the waves, or floating on my back. How I loved the water!

While on this holiday I met a blind lady who was staying at the same boarding house. Every morning she went for a long swim with her companion, usually venturing about two miles. She was full of a certain brand of exuberance for life and was, I thought, able to do far more without her sight than many people did with it. In the afternoons she knitted at great speed, produced some superb crocheting and occupied herself in reading from braille.

I tried to imagine what life would be like without sight. Keeping my eyes tightly closed, I walked across the beach for a few yards only to stub my toe painfully on some large pebbles. Young as I was I was very thankful for the benefit of my sight and strong body.

However, that holiday, that summer, was my last summer of physical freedom, as fate was to deal out a very painful blow which was to change the entire direction of the rest of my life.

2 Hospital life

It was June 1950, a stiflingly hot summer, when the nights were long and suffocating and even a cotton sheet felt like a fur rug.

My swimming and dancing activities were paramount in my life. The dancing school which I attended had just put on their summer show, and I vividly remember we wore ghastly white dresses with huge red spots and an enormous red and white spotted bow in our hair. We rehearsed most evenings before shows, usually giving one performance at our local town hall and another at the local old people's home.

I remember that particular week how I plodded to school. That hill that I had climbed so many times before seemed steeper than ever. My legs ached miserably and frequently felt weak. Too much dancing, everybody said, you have strained yourself.

I went to the Mother Superior and asked to be excused from all sports that week. She said that I had 'growing pains', whatever they may be, and so on I had to plod.

I was even too tired and achy to swim. It was quite usual for me to swim in the open air pool, often getting there at 6.30 in the morning for training, and spending hours in the water. I usually went with a crowd of friends and we used to throw pennies into the water at the deep end and dive for them. Most of the summer holidays were spent at the pool. I used to continue going right through until late October when it closed for the winter, and I was so tough that I often swam when frost was on the ground and the water temperature at freezing point.

The pains in my legs and spine worsened, and I took to my bed willingly – anything to escape those painful weak legs. Despite resting in bed, things became worse, I started to lose control of my bladder, and our local doctor queried 'rheumatic fever', but as that day wore on I began to lose the use of my legs and was hurriedly admitted into an isolation hospital.

My brother, Tony, still recalls that day as vividly as if it were yesterday, although he was only five at the time. It was actually 11 June, my Dad's birthday, and there was I, plump, strong and suntanned, being carried down the staircase on a stretcher.

The days that followed are hazy. I was in a single room in an isolation hospital in Tottenham, north London, and in my sickness dreamed that I was being swept all over London by a little man with a huge broom.

Up and down pavements we went, through bumpy cobbled alleyways and up and down hills. At one time he swept me through a huge pile of broken glass, and laughed about it, until my exhausted pain-racked body could stand no more, and that day passed. I looked out of the window from my small room and it was a beautiful June morning, the pain was gone, no more delirious dreams, but there was no movement at all in my right leg and little in my left. It was impossible to sit up. I tried desperately to raise my head from the pillow, but nothing happened. Weeks later I learned that I had polio; there had been an epidemic that year and thousands had been struck down by this disabling and often fatal illness.

Disability in childhood brings with it its own anaesthetic, as you live in a sublime fantasy world, believing that next week or the week after you will be back to normal again, swimming, dancing, running. There was no thought that this could be for the rest of my life.

Hospital life was disciplined and a lot of the nurses had a very hard approach to the children in that Isolation Unit. As the weeks went on I was exercised, had terribly painful experiences with the physiotherapist who stretched my useless leg in an attempt to try to prevent the wasting in my muscles, and I was able to sit propped with pillows. Within a month my left leg had regained much of its strength and I was able to put my foot out of bed and feel the wooden floor beneath me. That was a great feeling, a contact with reality. My right leg refused to obey any commands. It flopped uselessly at my side rather like the limp swaying movements of a rag doll and my entire spine was stiff and agonisingly painful. If I moved a burning searing pain seemed to start in the base of my spine and continue up to the nape of my neck. My leg did not look very different from the other one apart from having an odd blueish tinge because of the defective circulation.

I was moved from the isolation hospital to a dreadful place way out in the country which was run by an order of nuns and was more like an army camp. The so-called ward in which I was placed had actually been used for long-term tuberculosis patients. It was a huge converted cowshed, with a pull-across sliding tarpaulin curtain which was closed at night and wide open all day during the summer months. Obviously, this 'fresh air treatment' had been used for TB cases years back.

How I hated that place! Nothing much was done to help my condition, nor that of anybody else; day after day we lay in bed, no treatment was offered, food and drink was served to us on tin plates and tin mugs. I never was so lonely in my life as I was in that hospital. I pined for my mother in particular and the rest of my family to such an extent that I felt as if I had a gaping hole in the pit of my stomach.

Visiting was once a week only on a Sunday afternoon, just two precious hours – it took nearly a day for my parents to get there by public transport. How we longed for that visiting afternoon, counting the hours to Sunday, and then when it came we were too choked with emotion and dread of separation to enjoy it.

How very different today, now that the medical profession has realised that children need their families more when they are ill, not less. Within a few weeks my father had arranged a move for me to Westminster Children's Hospital in London. It was great there, the nurses were kind and understanding, and I had a view over busy London during the day. But as I needed long-term care, this busy hospital could not keep me and once again I was transferred, this time to the orthopaedic hospital in Stanmore.

I remember that hospital and the ward – Coxen Children's Ward – as if it were yesterday. The hospital was vast and stood in acres of ground. The buildings were ancient and sparse, and in the ward where I was a section of the roof was dome-shaped with glass panels. If it rained you were kept awake by the pattering on the glass roof above and when it was sunny the ward became unbearably hot.

There were rows and rows of beds and at the very end of the ward near to the office was a further huge area with row upon row of large white cots, filled with the pathetic sight of tiny tots in various positions, in spinal jackets, frog plasters, plaster beds, traction beds. Some poor little mites were strapped to a terrible contraption which resembled a crucifix. I learned that this was to try to correct spinal deformities.

I worked hard in the physiotherapy department at Stanmore. There was very little lying in bed. I was exercised, massaged, given electric treatment to try to stimulate some response to the muscles in my right leg, and made to lift weights with my left leg in order to build up maximum strength. It was sheer delight when I found that the physiotherapy department had a swimming pool, and even more exciting to find that once in the water I could swim nearly as well as before. After months of immobility I almost wished that I could remain in water for the rest of my life. Often I would escape into my fantasy world, away from all the pain and suffering and frustration, imagining that I had changed into a mermaid and met a handsome merman. Together we dived to the depths of the sea, lived in a beautiful cave surrounded by coral, and raised a big family. All too soon my fantasy world faded and I had to face the stark realities of hospital life. The wheels of the beds had to face inwards, counterpanes were turned down

15 inches at the top, and only one toy or book was allowed on the bed at a time, because, we were told, cluttered beds made the ward look untidy. Great attention was paid to nursing the body, but there the healing stopped: nobody considered that the body had a mind and a soul.

Dressed in dark navy with white collar and cuffs, a large silver buckle at the waist and a tall stiffly starched hat, Matron used to pay a daily visit followed by her stream of disciples, and as they walked through each ward they resembled a slithering snake. Matron had a very grim expression. I never did see her smile and we all rather held our breath until she had gone. I think the nurses did too.

Very shortly after my admission to Stanmore I was placed in a wheelchair and shown how to manoeuvre myself about. The tremendous strength I had built up in my shoulders from all the exercise and swimming I had done proved its value and I was soon careering about with great speed and efficiency.

The little girl in the next bed to mine went home, and within a short period a new boy arrived. He was called Charlie. When he was admitted he was very ill and I remember him going to the operating theatre and coming back on a trolley looking as white as a corpse. I was sure he was going to die as he had a blood transfusion in one arm and a drip in the other and looked so deathly white and silent. Within a few days he seemed better but had to face up to the fact that his left leg had been amputated as the result of a serious road accident. He cried for days and so did his mum and dad, and when he realised that he would never play football again, he threw his breakfast tray across the floor.

Charlie was eight with bright auburn hair and a freckled face, and I was 10, but we were soon inseparable, and indeed I really think we fell in love with each other. He called me 'Plaits'. He was very quickly got out of bed and put into a wheelchair in which he became super-efficient. We used to have races in the grounds, until the day that he became a little too enthusiastic and landed on the ground with his chair on top of him. From that day on Charlie and I were confined to the limitations of the corridor, which was not half as much fun. We did our school work together, we did crossword puzzles, I read him stories as he was not able to read very well, and we talked about what we would do when we grew up and got married. He did not have a left leg and my right leg was useless, so together we would be complete.

Every day Charlie and I were picked up by ambulance and taken to the physiotherapy department, which was quite a way from the hospital wards. Before we went we were put into enormous hospital baths, great galvanised steel monstrosities standing on four large feet, so deep that when you were put in only your head appeared over the top. The baths were cleaned with a very coarse abrasive powder, so as you sat in the water the residue of granules stung your bottom. You washed yourself with a piece of hard, maroon-coloured hospital soap with a carbolic smell so strong that your skin looked like crumpled parchment when you came out. You dried yourself on huge, very stiff, rough towels, rather like wrapping your body in sandpaper. There were really very few comforts, just the basic necessities for survival, but the physiotherapy and rehabilitation units were good, and with dogged determination they made every moving part that did work, function to its maximum potential.

During my long period in hospital a little seed was sown which slowly grew into the realisation that people and healing were going to become the dominant factors in my life. As I wheeled myself down the rows and rows of cots and saw such suffering in tiny tots, I felt such compassion and sometimes anger at God for letting such innocents suffer. I would stroke a hot head, clasp a tiny fist and wonder why these awful things had to happen, even to babies. The nights were always long and disturbed by the crying of sad and lonely children, but on Tuesdays – operation day – the night sounds were very different; children were now suffering real pain after surgery and there never seemed to be enough nurses to be with them.

When I think of today's hospital care for children, with mothers actually allowed to stay and nurse their own child and in many instances sleep at the hospital, there really is no comparison between nursing care and attention today and what I experienced 39 years ago.

The nurses used to work very hard, doing lots of physical cleaning as well as nursing the sick. The wooden floor in the ward was scrubbed at least twice a week, and I can remember so clearly the ward maids coming in with their steel buckets and large scrubbing brushes attached by a wooden handle. The nurses would push the beds to the right-hand side of the ward and then the scrubbing would begin. The ward maids struggled to lift those heavy buckets which were full of steaming soapy water with a strong smell of disinfectant. If they plonked their buckets down under the glass dome of the roof and the sun was out, I would start day-dreaming again: the soapy white bubbles would become billowing floating clouds, and there was I flying through the clouds with the grace of a bird, no useless leg and clumsy body. Maybe I would fly away to heaven,where I would not need a physical body,yet most of all I wanted to stay on earth to be with my family. In any case I would miss Charlie.

The sound of continuous scrubbing broke my dreams and it was back to Coxen Ward and the hospital life that I had become quite used to. It was quite obvious after five months that I was never going to be able to walk again without a support for my leg, and it was decided to fit my right leg with a caliper. At the same time Charlie went for a fitting for his artificial leg. Within a few weeks we had both had fittings, but while we waited for these limbs to appear we started walking between parallel bars, then progressed to crutches.

Eventually both monstrosities arrived. I often wondered if the people who made the calipers would have ever been prepared to wear them, as they were heavy, unsightly supports, with lots of leather straps and steel bars at each side of your leg which fitted into your shoe.

We had to be taught how to get out of a chair, how to climb a few stairs with the use of a hand rail on one side and walking stick on the other, how to get in and out of a bath – that was a job. The most difficult thing of all was learning to get yourself off the floor after a fall, and we had many. I always felt like an overturned beetle. Charlie and I made good progress in those hardworking weeks, receiving many bruises and bumps as we progressed to some sort of independence – he with his artificial leg and two sticks, and me with my caliper and crutches. Where there is a will there is a way, so they say, and we went backwards and forwards to the rehabilitation unit every day until we were able to master some of the everyday hurdles which we would encounter when we went back to the outside world.

At the end of a session in the rehabilitation unit we were exhausted. I used to long for bed where I could remove the caliper and free myself from the discomfort and chafing it caused. I quite frequently had a circle of blisters around my thigh which had to be bandaged overnight so that I could go 'back to work' the next day.

I really cannot look back on my hospital life as a dreadful experience. You very quickly become institutionalised when the confines of the hospital are all you know and you soon forget the outside world. Even your immediate family seem to fade because hospital life takes over, and you are surrounded by so many people for whom disability is the norm. It is much easier to cope with disability in an orthopaedic hospital where the needs of the physically handicapped are managed in an environment where there are no stairs or hills to climb and where everything is geared to make life as easy as possible. The real problems begin when you have to adapt to life with one leg in a normal world where you are pitied and isolated from society, because you are different.

3 The confines of freedom

By December 1950 I was home, the home that I had thought about, imagined, counted the days to, but I hated it. It was home to a wheelchair which took up too much space in our small living room and to the pitying glances from old friends.

Even though a wheelchair was available, there was no more racing up and down the corridors with Charlie who, shortly before I left, had another operation for an infected thigh bone. I missed Charlie even more when he wrote me a very scribbled postcard saying: 'Dear Plaits, Nuffins going right and I miss you tons and tons, Luv Charlie.' No children, chatter, drama, swimming pool. There could be no more tearing off for a swim with a towel over one shoulder and costume over the other, and there were going to be problems in getting back to some sort of education.

The rooms at home were small and claustrophobic. There was a very steep flight of stairs up to my bedroom and the bathroom and toilet. That was the first hurdle. During the first few days I was carried up and down, but I soon got fed up with that and eventually managed by humping myself up and down on my bottom.

Twice a week I was picked up by ambulance and taken to the out-patients department of the orthopaedic hospital in London where I had massage, exercise and electrical treatment. The next battle was getting back to school. For a while I had a teacher at home, then discussions with the education authorities raised the question of my going to a school for the physically handicapped. My mother and father strongly disagreed. It would have been a disaster as the standard of education at these schools was so low that unfortunately one was almost labelled for life.

The convent was not very happy about having me back, as I suppose I was considered rather a liability, but after some persuasion it was agreed that I should return in the spring of 1951. I was taken to school in a wheelchair, and my poor mother had to push me – no lightweight – up a very steep hill.

Everything was difficult, manoeuvring myself up those slippery polished wooden stairs, being stared at as if I was a monster with four heads, slippery corridors where I often fell, and missing out on all the activities I loved best: the sports, dancing, running. Every day was a constant physical and mental battle, and often my days ended in bad temper, with me wanting to vent my feelings and tear and destroy things. A good scream would probably have done me a power of good, but that would have been unacceptable in my family, who, though they did their best for me, had no idea of the frustration, anger and the tremendous adjustments I was trying to make. I wish they could have allowed me to be angry and not have expected 'the stiff upper lip' British approach to tragedy. I know now that the suppression of my feelings led to very severe allergic rhinitis and skin eruptions, which was something else to put up with. My family were only happy with me when I was nice and happy and smiling – a tall order – and if I was bad-tempered or difficult, I would return home to a cold silence, a withdrawal of love, which was another punishment. I am sure they were unaware of what they were doing to me and I know that accepting my disability was, in many ways, just as painful for them as it was for me.

I always felt sorry for my brother during these early years. I am sure he missed out on a lot of attention as my needs were always to the fore. Tony was such a quiet, nervous little boy, with an aura of spirituality surrounding him which developed in intensity during his adult years. My father never did understand his individuality and could not accept that he really was quite uninterested in football, cricket or similar team activities. He did not even mix much with the children at school, he much preferred fishing, or rowing or any of the similar solitary pursuits. He clung to my mother for the gentleness and understanding he craved and which she alone was able to provide for him. There was a tremendous bond between the two of them which still remains today.

My schooling at the convent proceeded along the usual routines. The problems remained, but school friends volunteered to take turns in taking me to school which was a relief for my poor mother. When I was 13 a new music teacher joined the school, who was not within the order of nuns. Her name was Miss May. She and I got on very well from the word go. She appreciated my love of music and suggested giving me extra lessons in singing after school. And so the lessons began and what proved to be for me the beginning of years and years of joy, the development of a certain inner strength and the opportunity for self-expression.

My debut was at school when we portrayed a Dutch scene. Dressed in wide brown baggy trousers with a checked tunic top, I sang 'Baggy

Breeches'. I can remember each and every one of those words and notes as if it were yesterday. Today I possess a large suitcase packed with musical scores, recitals, light operetta, and I can still pick any one at random and remember all the notes, timing and words. I studied each and every one in such detail that they are still stored away in a computerised section of my brain.

I really looked forward to my two hours a week in the large school hall with the grand piano that shone so brightly with the years of constant polishing that you could see your reflection as clearly as in a mirror. I started with simple madrigal folk songs and light songs from the shows and within a year had advanced to Strauss, Lehar, Gilbert and Sullivan which was always a great favourite.

Miss May took a great interest in me, always encouraging me to develop, study and understand music. She will never know how important a role she played in my life, even if she only directed me along the right road.

By the time I was 15 I was really quite mobile. No further life or strength had returned to my leg and hip, but I had learned how to cope with it, had mastered getting on and off buses, walking with just one stick, and my wheelchair was a thing of the past.

I had even returned to outdoor swimming. The problem was getting in and out of the pool as without my caliper my leg was a useless floppy limb, upon which I could put no weight. However, I used to shuffle along on the ground until I got to the poolside and then hurl myself over the side. The only problem was that I wore the bottom out of my swimsuits! Once in the water I escaped from the confines of my disability, and experienced freedom of body, mind and spirit. Here in the water I was totally in control, as the water gave me support and movement without any strain. I swam on top of and underneath the water. My lung capacity was huge from the development of muscle in my singing training, and I was able to swim the entire length under water. Eventually I built up my training until I was able to swim 1½ miles, and this I did every time I went to the pool.

My poor leg did not take much to being put into the cold water, especially when summer turned to autumn and the pool temperature was very low. Circulatory problems in polio are a real problem. However, I preferred to limp home with one blue frozen leg rather than miss out on what I enjoyed most.

Eventually I became 'accepted' at school as a normal person with a gammy leg. I had been put in charge of the dining-room during lunch time and was expected to keep a watchful eye on the infants and juniors to make sure they ate all their lunch. Wasted food was a mortal sin, but as the meals in the convent were generally uneatable I am quite sure that if any Local Authority Inspector had visited our dining-room and seen the quality of the food that we were expected to eat, there would have been some questions to answer.

Whenever we had a school fête, or any fund-raising scheme, we as pupils were expected to bring in cakes, which were then sold. Our dessert for the next fortnight was the left-over cakes which got staler and staler until they were like bricks. A very thin watery custard was poured over and that was what we had to eat. The slogan 'Fête day, cake fortnight' made us all laugh until the tears rolled down our faces.

I could not bear to see the little ones sitting in front of these dreadful meals for over an hour at a time while the nuns scolded and complained about the waste. Outside the dining-room window was a large water butt which collected rainwater from the gutters above, and so with great speed I would lean out of the window and scrape all the left over food into the butt. I then returned the empty plates to the kitchen much to the relief of the infants and the satisfaction of the nuns. I repeated this procedure for many months and nothing was noticed until the following summer when the heat of the sun on the water butt made the contents become foul and the smell was so strong that investigations were made and I had to own up to my unforgivable sin. I was sent to Reverend Mother who severely reprimanded me and reminded me that had I been a Catholic I could have gone to confession to ask for forgiveness, but as I was an 'outsider' – well, there really was no hope for me. My punishment was sorting out the stationery cupboard and learning several prayers by heart which had to be repeated a week later to Reverend Mother.

I still think that my actions were justified. The food was not fit for human consumption and it was wrong to expect young childen to eat it regardless. The main problem associated with the Catholic religion in my experience is that it is a religion based on fear. In the same breath we were taught about a kind loving God who watched over us all, yet as soon as we did anything wrong we had to live in fear of him and dread that when we died we would go into the fires of hell. I thought real love was unconditional!

The most important thing about disability is accepting that once everything possible has been done for you, or it, you have to learn to live with the problem. It is futile to go on longing and hoping for a miracle to occur, for they seldom do. Yet miracles can happen when you develop every single aspect of your entire being, when you make the most of every single skill or talent that has been given to you and go out and face the world. Eventually you will be accepted not as a 'disabled person', but as a normal individual with all the hopes, wishes, emotions and fears of anybody else, only you have a gammy leg. I intended to make my mark in life. Today, thank God, disabled people have far more help than ever before, mobility allowances so that they can have independence and the freedom of driving, training schemes and jobs are available, and parking facilities help to give easy access.

If I could bestow two wishes on a new baby, apart from the gift of good health, I would wish it courage and the determination to face life. Courage has nothing whatsoever to do with rescuing somebody from the jaws of death – that we do on impulse without thought; courage is conquering the unknown things and in meeting the smaller challenges of everyday life.

Teenage years were inevitably difficult; I did have friends but obviously they were off and about doing all the things that I would have loved to have done but which were impossible, so I was, in effect, left behind.

I did join the British Polio Fellowship, and took part in their many social activities, and I made some good friends. Here I met people with disabilities of all levels, some completely chairbound, some with partial paralysis of a single limb, some with calipers and sticks. Some were very sour and resentful about the blow that fate had dealt them, but many led good, full, active and useful lives and many young disabled couples got together and married. It was a fine organisation that gave many disabled people the opportunity for travel, crafts and outings which they would probably never have had previously.

When I used to meet so many at the monthly meetings, it always hit home to me that all this disability and suffering was caused by a minute virus which did all its dirty work in twelve short hours.

My two main loves were still swimming and my music. Miss May was quite confident that I could make a career of singing if I wished. The only other subject that I excelled in was English. My English teacher said I should develop the skill of writing and take the subject seriously, but at that time I just did everything for the love of it. Even at that very early age, I was aware of a powerful energy in my diaphragm area which surfaced when I sang, or when I got down to writing; and in later years it increased until eventually I was able to channel it into the true direction for which it was intended.

4 Nightingale and legal eagles

In the spring of 1955 I decided to take my musical interest more seriously. A good friend introduced me to Marion Walters, who had been a teacher at the Guildhall School of Music for many years and now had a school in north London where she taught singing.

I shall never forget that first interview. Marion was a very elegant woman in her mid-fifties with luxuriant silver grey hair piled up into a bun. She had a warm, outgoing personality and a great joy of living that revealed itself when she sang in her fine soprano voice. Marion was married to Ivor, a Welshman with an equally fine tenor voice. Their entire lives had been devoted to music, in their early years as concert singers and latterly as teachers.

Marion taught me how to recite poetry, how to stand, how to breathe deeply into the pit of the stomach; 'Remember to sing with your soul', she would say, and I did. I loved every minute of every lesson. Music was as easy for me to learn as breathing and Marion could not have had a more enthusiastic pupil.

After my first 18 months as a student I began working for the London Musical Festivals. These were nerve-racking but challenging experiences, although I must admit that after you had heard the same piece of music sung 25 times, it did become rather boring, particularly if you were number 25! After the class was finished the two judges would get together and deal out the marks. I won the Silver Rose Bowl in the Gilbert and Sullivan class when I sang 'The Sun Whose Rays' from *The Mikado*, a silver medal in the madrigal class, and a gold medal when I sang the soprano lead in the Nuns' Chorus.

I joined a concert choir through which I made some good friends. We used to go out on Saturday evenings giving concerts, sometimes to hospitals, sometimes to old people's homes, and sometimes we were engaged for private functions.

School was quite a bore now that I was 15. The only subjects taught were the most basic. We did not even learn human biology apart from the life and mating habits of frogs and stick insects. I am sure that I could have been interested in any practical subject – home economics, or some sort of craft – other than needlework.

I really believe that the nuns imagined that each of us girls would emerge into the life of a lady in which you moved in just the right social circles, spent your mornings writing absolutely perfect letters to your wide circle of friends, your afternoons doing fine needlework, and on Sundays spent your entire day going backwards and forwards to church. I wonder how many of us had the opportunity or the inclination for that sort of life?

Looking back on those five years from the day I contracted polio, I think I learned a great deal about life from a very early age. Those early years had been hard suffering years but I had ignited in me a little flame that assured me that I was going to beat this rotten illness and lead a full and enriching life. I was determined to do more with my life with one leg than the average person does with two.

After leaving school I went to Pitman's College to study shorthand, typing and book-keeping, English and maths. Obviously I was going to have to choose a career where I was sitting down most of the time. If it had not been for polio I would have chosen a career in the medical world: nurse, social worker or something in the caring field where people mattered. However, I enjoyed the shorthand, found the typing fun, and soon achieved good speeds.

Our teacher was an elderly man whose name I cannot now remember. He was very tall, picked his nose a lot and had a set of badly fitting dentures which moved as he talked. However, he was a good teacher, which was the main thing. The college was small and personal and I was able to get to it by bus, even though it was just two stops. Sometimes on energetic days I walked.

By day I went to college and in the evenings I had my music, lines to learn, scores to study, timing to check. Every Tuesday night we rehearsed with the concert choir, so my life was a full one. The main area in my life where I achieved the greatest sensitivities were in the fields of communication: speaking, singing, writing. Whenever I was miserable I would go to the water for consolation. Swimming under water really does enable you to escape. At that young age I was unaware what the future would hold for me or what I really wanted from life. My mother and I were close, but my relationship with my father had its reserves. I think I was always a little afraid of him, and we certainly did not have the relaxed relationship that I wanted. He never was able to come to terms with his formerly active daughter being restricted by the frustrations of a considerable disability, and maybe his lack of understanding at times, his detachment from me was in a way a suppression of his grief. I could not understand his reaction then, but I do now.

I therefore had to set out to prove myself, prove that I was capable of far more than a typist's job in a local government office where I would sit for about 40 years doing the same job, go grey early and have a bun, spectacles and a big bosom. I really feel that my father thought I would end up in just such a position, which for me would have been a fate worse than death.

Other than career prospects, like most other teenagers, I wanted to be needed and loved. I wanted marriage and I desperately wanted children. (Maybe I wanted children far more than I wanted marriage.) Disability brought its restrictions here. First I was unable to circulate in a young environment because most young people were out, dancing, playing sports and in fact doing all the things I could not do, and secondly most men – at least young men – would not have considered becoming involved with a disabled woman.

I left Pitman's College with good speeds in both shorthand and typing, a smattering of a knowledge of book-keeping which I still loathed, and a grounding in general office management.

My first interview was quite a terrifying experience. I had applied for a job as a junior shorthand-typist in a local solicitor's office. The first hurdle was a dingy flight of winding stairs which were difficult to manage. I then went into an equally dingy waiting room. The offices were Victorian and very neglected. The ancient gas fire popped constantly; it was surrounded by some ugly, lurid green tiles. The faded patterned carpet was threadbare and in many places had worn into holes. The single small window looked out on to dozens and dozens of old tiled roofs with ugly chimneys which belched out a thin spiral of grey smoke. The desks were heavy solid oak but were old and worn, and one could imagine that had they been able to speak, they would have great stories to relate.

Mr Mo was a typical Victorian-looking solicitor, with his wing collar, half-rimmed glasses, pocket watch, a carnation in his buttonhole and a dark clerical suit which looked as if it should have been cleaned months ago. He appeared to be very tense and had quite an abrupt, almost rude manner, so I did not think much of him. However the job was to work for his assistant, who seemed a friendly woman. I was told before I went in to address Mr Mo as 'Sir'.

Going into Sir's room was like stepping back 100 years. The room was slightly plusher, with a crimson carpet that did not have any holes, an enormous old desk, and the walls were lined with deep shelves on which were bundled hundreds of old parchment documents, tied up with red silk ribbon. It smelled old and musty. Sir was a chain-smoker and a thick haze of yellow smoke billowed about the ceiling; he could not bear the windows open as he was very sensitive to draughts, so the atmosphere was absolutely putrid.

Sir wanted a trainee legal secretary to work 9–6 and alternate Saturday mornings for £3.10s per week – a fortune! There would be two weeks' paid holiday a year and he said that he did not accept 'illness' very favourably: 'I hope you are not going to fall down the stairs as you have a problem with your leg.' He said that it was hardly ever known for him to be away sick. I found this hard to believe when I looked at the dozens of stubs in his ashtray, and he had the most dreadful cough. 'I have several youngsters to see this afternoon,' he said, 'and by the way I hope you are good at English and can spell – I don't want to have to spend my time correcting letters.' I informed him that English was my subject, that I was excellent at spelling and quite capable of putting a business letter together.

I got the job and started work the following Monday morning. The law was far more interesting than I had imagined. I loved typing the legal documents on the pale blue oily parchment paper, sewing in any inner pages with green silk and finishing off with a blob of red sealing wax to secure the knot. There was much to learn, first of all in the probate department with all the wills and winding up of large estates, then on to conveyancing, litigation and eventually criminology.

Sir's bark proved to be far worse than his bite, and although he was a very uptight, insecure man, he did at times have quite a sense of humour. If he won his case it was smiles all round. If he lost, he growled around for days on end, demanded endless cups of tea which I made and then went out to buy his favourite buns with pink icing.

I got on very well there. I learned quickly and Mr Mo suggested that provided I could cope with the travelling, I should go up to the Lincoln's Inn branch for six months in order to get some first-hand experience of court work and criminology. They were really interesting months. I used to visit Somerset House and the Old Bailey, and became aware of the many problems humanity created for itself.

When I reached the age of 18 my salary went up to £6 which was thought quite considerable. Sir's secretary had left to have a baby and he offered me her job. It was just as well that I had a good command of written and spoken English as Sir's spelling and English were appalling, and his letter-writing left much to be desired.

I very diplomatically suggested that if he gave me the content of the letters I would write them myself, thus saving a lot of his valuable time. He sniffed and coughed at this prospect, smoked a few extra cigarettes that morning while he thought about it, but eventually decided that it was a good idea. From that day on I relieved him of a problem and earned a soft spot in his otherwise hard exterior.

I enjoyed my job, although we did work hard and in conditions that nobody would put up with today: dreadful old typewriters, a small cloakroom with a tiny little handbasin in which you were expected to wash cups as well as your hands, and only one cold tap which made quite loud exploding noises as you turned it on and sometimes emitted light brown rusty-coloured water. When you pulled the lavatory chain, which was solid brass with a white china handle painted with roses (quite a valuable asset today, I should think), the whole building trembled, almost as if in revolt.

By now I had expanded my social life by taking up more interests with the British Polio Fellowship. I joined various functions and activities, theatre visits and made many good friends.

During Christmas 1957 I was given the golden opportunity of singing the soprano lead in Bach's St Matthew Passion, Mendelssohn's 'Elijah' and Handel's 'Messiah' in the Central Hall, Westminster. It was a frightening but enthralling experience and one that I shall never forget. The vastness and superb acoustics of that large hall were perfect to sing in, and with the combination of three large choirs – in all about 300 voices – it was a momentous occasion.

Marion, my teacher, was still intent on me considering a professional career but I felt that it would be easier, and likely to cause far fewer complications, if I kept it as an enjoyable hobby. To me music was the ultimate expression of my inner self, it was demanding, exacting and needed self-discipline, but it gave me an inner peace. I feel that through music one becomes 'in tune with the infinite'; all one's frustrations, disability and sadness melt away in music. It is surely a great mental therapy.

In the spring of 1958 I left the legal profession to work for a large commercial concern. This was a bad move in one way, but completely changed the course of my life in another. The job was very well-paid but proved deadly boring, compared with the people-orientated job I had left. I never did find typing about the retail trade very inspiring, and although I was secretary to one of the directors and had a fine, comfortable, centrally heated office with a new typewriter and a super desk with a leather top, I somehow missed the popping gas fire, Sir's cough and the legal atmosphere. I was also engaged to work for the company accountant and that was how I met John.

5 All for love

John was the company accountant. He was also disabled as the result of polio. Though he had a considerable spinal deformity he was very ambulant and able to drive a car, which solved most of his mobility problems. Our common experience set up an instant friendship between us, and over lunch in the dining room the day after I joined the firm we found to our amazement that we lived only three miles from each other. He had actually been in the same children's ward in the same hospital one year later than I.

Polio had struck him at the tender age of three. He had been away on holiday with friends who also had young children, and had shared a bed with a little boy who went to bed with a high temperature and aching legs. Twenty-four hours later the little boy recovered, but John contracted polio – the other boy had the non-paralytic type.

John had a very restricted childhood and at the age of 11 went into the orthopaedic hospital in Stanmore for major surgery, to try to correct the severe curvature in his spine. After months and months of lying in a plaster bed, he finally returned home to spend most of his day lying flat in a spinal carriage. He was never allowed to sit for more than three hours at a time, so had to be pushed to school by his mother in his spinal carriage, sit for three hours at a desk, then spend another hour flat before he could continue with his work.

Although he was 15 years my senior, we had a great deal in common. He had such a fine brain and to have achieved the status of a Chartered Accountant was certainly something.

John's parents were alive. His mother, Hilda, was an absolute dear who had sacrificed everything for her beloved son. She had suffered mental agonies during his long complicated major surgical operations – he had three major spinal operations in 18 months. Her whole aim was for her son to use his brilliant brain and make something of his life, despite polio, despite his deformity, despite everything.

John's father, Sid, was a weak man who could offer no support to his son either emotionally or financially and had taken to drink, maybe in an attempt to drown his sorrows. There had never been any money available for any comforts or benefits for the family, as it was all spent at the local pub. When John matriculated with honours and obtained a place at Cambridge University, there was not even enough money available to pay the small percentage of the fees required, so John had to forgo that opportunity, which was a tremendous disappointment, and get his accountancy qualification by working for years and years as an articled clerk at a salary of £2 a week.

John's mother went out cleaning as she was absolutely determined to save enough money for her son to have a car, so that he would be able to get about with little effort.

John was also secretary to the British Polio Fellowship. He belonged to a different branch from the one I attended, but I remembered seeing his name on the letterheads of the Fellowship.

We were obviously instantly attracted to each other. We had both suffered, missed out on a lot of fun in our childhood and we had both triumphed over our disabilities. John was such a positive character, I never ever heard him complain or grumble about his illness. He had the same love of music as I had, so we started going out and about to concerts in London, and oh, what luxury to be picked up for work in the mornings! No more slipping on the ice and landing on your backside, no more getting soaked in the rain, and certainly no frustration in being unable to run for a bus.

We went for long drives in the country at weekends, visiting stately homes and gardens, and eventually I was introduced to his sister and her husband who lived in a small village just a little way from Brighton. They lived in a truly picturesque tiny cottage with a real quarry-tiled floor, Aga cooker, a stable door and roses that really grew around the door.

Despite our close friendship, I had to leave that job in commerce and go back into the law, where people mattered and there seemed some purpose and satisfaction in what you did.

I joined another, much larger firm of solicitors, again in north London but with several branches elsewhere. Back I went into the atmosphere of court hearings and the musty smell of old dusty documents that I loved. To go into court with the gowned and wigged judges, and to listen to all the legal paraphernalia was like stepping back in time. Some of the cases were tragic, and any case in which assault of children was involved left me nauseated and revolted by the inhumanity of man. Plenty of almost inhuman acts were committed upon innocent children and I am sure there were plenty more that never came to court. It seemed the easiest thing in the world to give birth, but many parents proved totally inadequate when it came to the full-time commitment of rearing children. Others were able to cope with physical care but emotional needs were sadly neglected. I am sure that children would far prefer to be loved and dirty than live in a sterile, cold environment lacking any kind of affection or communication.

My increased involvement with the British Polio Fellowhip thanks to my friendship with John and his position as Secretary within that society led me to meet still more people who had achieved so much with so little. When I met and worked with people in the normal active world who complained and grumbled about little mundane frustrations I quickly became intolerant. When I met up with those restricted to life in a wheelchair, yet still eager to compete in sporting activities, swimming, table tennis, archery, even netball, I thanked God that my disability had allowed me still to be able to walk, even with difficulty.

I have seen beautiful works of art achieved by polio victims who have little or no use in their arms and hold paintbrushes between their toes. A great friend of mine, Sylvia, had been chairbound since the age of three. She was completely paralysed from her neck down, and had little movement in her hands. Yet she wrote many articles for magazines and eventually a book called *Toes to the Grindstone,* which she wrote by typing with her toes.

Accepting limitations and yet making the most of one's capabilities is perhaps the hardest part of a disability. The adjustment must be made without giving way to circumstances too much, with a certain toughness of character and yet without bitterness against the way life has turned out. Nor is it a task that is over once and for all – like learning to ride a bike or swim. It is a constant effort to keep on an even keel. One wants neither pity nor concessions on account of the handicap and yet, to a greater or lesser degree, it is always present and one must accept the fact.

Seeing the activities and creativity people have developed despite disability gets your priorities into the right place, and therefore I have little or no time for people who complain and who blame life for their failures, who constantly say 'if only' or 'I never had the opportunity', and I become very angry when I meet those who have everything to live for, but have no real appreciation of anything.

To have a brain that can command a body into whatever action is desired of it should give one the basis to lead a happy, active, fulfilled life, but I have often found the reverse to be true. When one's body is restricted or damaged and limited in movement, one often seems to develop finer qualities and abilities than would otherwise have been revealed.

John and I made close friends with another young couple, June and

John. They had both contracted polio as young children and had met through the society. June was such a pretty girl. Though she had to spend a good deal of her time in a wheelchair, there was very little she could not do. She managed to do all her own housework, got herself and wheelchair into her own hand-controlled Mini and was expert at indoor bowls. We often used to go with them for a match, and June always won. John was a warm loving man, who just walked with a slight limp so he was able to hold down a very good job as a book-keeper. During the years that we knew them, they produced two daughters, just one year apart. June would tuck a baby down at the side of her wheelchair, manoeuvre herself into the bathroom and bath and change the baby. With the speed of light she would then manoeuvre herself from the bathroom out to the garden where she put the baby in the pram. In the afternoons she would get herself and baby into the car, put the baby on the back seat strapped into a carrycot and off she would go to shop. The shop-keepers all knew June well and loved this pretty, brave little woman, and one of the assistants would keep a weather eye on the baby while June was in the shop.

They were such a happy couple and really loved each other for what they were, strong, capable and brave. June's girls grew up into fine young women and we had a lasting friendship with them for years. Tragically her husband John died from kidney failure in his fifties and I lost contact with June, despite efforts to find out where she went after his death.

At Christmas 1959 John took me to see the superb D'Oyly Carte production of *The Mikado*, the story of a Japanese girl in love. The Japanese heroine reminded John of another heroine in an oriental play, Lady 'Precious Stream', and on my Christmas card that month was written 'To my Lady Precious Stream for ever, John'. From that happy Christmas I became aware of a growing need to spend my life with John, despite our disabilities, the age difference, what our parents would say, the fact that I was only 19. Despite everything we became engaged on my nineteenth birthday. My parents justifiably could see many difficulties ahead and were not too pleased, but I knew that we shared a mutual understanding and wanted to spend our lives together.

I was lucky in that we would be able to start our married life in our own home and not in rented accommodation. We spent several months looking for a flat or maisonette. It was necessary for us to remain in north London because of our jobs, and eventually we found the right place, a large flat in Edmonton. We really wanted a ground-floor flat, but as this seemed impossible to find at that time, and as this first home would probably be a stopgap before looking for a bungalow, we settled for a first-floor maisonette.

The address was Regal Court, although there was nothing at all regal about it. It was in a courtyard with parking in the front and a balcony which overlooked a railway line. The flat itself had two bedrooms, a large kitchen/dining room, a large lounge, bathroom and toilet. We paid £1,500 for it, which was a good average price for a flat in 1959!

Together we did a lot of decorating. I could not climb ladders but John could, so he dealt with the upper part of the rooms while I did all the lower areas. Together we made the perfect team. We painted, papered, hung pictures, curtains, bought curtains and furniture, and it very soon became a home.

And so Lady Precious Stream fell in love with and was to be loved by a man who adored her and valued every minute of their life together.

6 That was my lovely day

On 7 May 1960 John and I were married, two people who had experienced suffering, a tremendous physical setback, but in spite of that had made great strides in finding some purpose in life. I did love him, that I was sure of, but his love for me was totally unconditional. I always found it embarrassing when he told me that I was his life, and that he adored and worshipped the very ground I walked upon. Maybe at 20 these powerful emotions were a little beyond my understanding, while he, being 15 years older, perhaps had certain more mature feelings which I was not yet ready to cope with.

Our wedding day was one of those 'perfect hazy days', sunny and warm with a cloudless blue sky. Every bride is entitled to a magical fairy-tale wedding day, and I had it. We were married at the old local church in North London which I had belonged to since I was a little girl, attending Brownie meetings, Girl Guides, Sunday School, youth clubs: it was the church that I had sung in many a time.

All my friends and relatives were present, and the concert choir which I had belonged to for so many years sang for us. It was lovely to see the familiar faces of those 30 people who had become good friends of ours over the years. I had asked for 'Oh Rejoice that the Lord has Arisen' from *Cavalleria Rusticana*, and as the sun shone brilliantly through those beautiful stained-glass windows it seemed as if there was indeed something to glory about.

We had a reception in a large hall for about 80 guests and later an evening reception which we held in our garden at home and which went on until very late in the evening. We had so many lovely presents, good wishes, cards and telegrams from so many people – a happy and joyous start to our life together.

The following day we went off to a small olde-worlde hotel in Dedham, Suffolk. I remember it was called 'Le Talbooth' – quite THE place to stay in. Dedham is a typical English country village in true 'Constable country', and we visited Flatford Mill, Ipswich and all the surrounding beauty spots. I am sure all the colours in the countryside that spring were far richer than ever before, or maybe I had looked at life before with less depth. Everything seemed so green and lush, and the spring flowers seemed more vivid and smelt better than ever.

The best part of having a unity with someone is the enjoyment of doing things together. There are very few things you can enjoy on your own. Even simple pleasures such as visiting the cinema are more enjoyable for a couple than for a single person. There is more pleasure in cooking a meal that someone else can enjoy with you, and more fun in saving up together for that special something. Loving means 'giving' – giving of yourself. Words can be so very cheap unless backed up by actions. It has to be unconditional and each partner must be allowed the freedom to develop mentally without feeling expected to be a carbon copy of the other.

The bonding of man and woman is the greatest force in life, for without it procreation would cease. And yet on reflection this strong emotion can cause no end of heartbreak, pain and suffering, but still we go on looking, hoping, trying to find the ultimate happiness in another fragile human being. This strong passion, this love and the heartbreak that comes from broken relationships have stimulated musicians and artists to create some of the most outstanding works of art, so from mental misery comes superb creativity, and all based on an indefinable feeling, an unrecognisable energy that indeed man has died for.

That was such a wonderful happy summer. We visited many friends who then came back to see us, we went to the coast, had long drives out into the country and made several trips to John's sister, Betty, and her husband Gwyn, a Welshman – in fact they were a lovely couple. They had a delightful little daughter of 15 months, Sarah, who had the most perfect round cherubic face and enormous blue eyes. She was quite adorable.

I had few domestic skills. My mother had really been too super-efficient, and the kitchen at home which was such a small one was her 'domain', so I hardly ever intruded except to wash up on occasions. John and I had quite a selection of beautifully browned chicken joints which were raw inside, potatoes that were either hard or cooked to a mush, burnt toast, and over-cooked everything. However, I learned fast and within three months was quite a good basic cook.

The perfect weather stretched into October. I love autumn, it means to me crunchy brown leaves, the most superb range of colours, colours in fact that I enjoy wearing, bonfires, apples and acorns, squirrels, the season of abundance. It was late October when my doctor confirmed that another abundance was in store and that I was pregnant. We were delighted, and this experience was to fulfil almost the most important need in my life. I had such a strong maternal drive that I would have been utterly devastated if I had been unable to conceive.

There is surely something very special about pregnancy, especially the first time. I seemed to go into a sort of 'hibernation state', feeling very tired all the time, very sick too, but also elated. If it had been socially acceptable to have sat on a warm nest for those first three and a half months I am sure I would have been quite happy to do so. I was unprepared for my overpowering protective feeling towards a minute speck of humanity that was hardly identifiable as yet. I remember John saying that in those first few early months I seemed to lose all reasoning and intellect. He laughed about it and called me his 'broody hen'.

I reverted to normal three months later, the sickness went, my energy returned and my brain began to function again, thank God. I think it was getting rather boring being married to a 'clucking hen'. At the first ante-natal examination it was discovered that I had high blood pressure, too high to leave untreated, and so I was admitted straight from the ante-natal department into the in-patient section.

The hospital was pretty grim, very busy with an enormous, very impersonal ante-natal ward. I was pretty annoyed at being in hospital so soon in pregnancy and also not keen on being prodded and poked by an army of medical students and nurses. Evidently the prospect of a polio victim giving birth was 'different', and obstetric problems were envisaged. One specialist said that I would in all probability have to have a Caesarian section; another said he could see no necessity.

I was in hospital that time for a month, on a strict weight-reducing diet with lots of bed-rest, and tablets to control the build-up of fluid which I somehow had floating around. I seemed to spend most of my day 'spending pennies' and actually did shed a stone in weight in just ten days. With the loss of this excess build-up of fluid my blood pressure dropped dramatically.

That month was about the longest in my life, even though I had lots of visitors and John visited every evening straight from the office. We named our baby Mark as we were both convinced that it would be a boy. I was discharged home shortly before Christmas, the last Christmas we would have as a couple; next year Mark would be with us and Christmas would take on an extra meaning.

We had a quiet family Christmas, with no Christmas pudding, mince pies or alcohol for me, but it did not seem to matter. I was more intent on keeping out of hospital. My ever-increasing lump became active by the month and I used to lie in bed at night wondering which end was where. There seemed to be a large bump under my ribs which I thought was maybe his head, or maybe his bottom, and often a small foot or fist would prod my side. It is still the greatest miracle as far as I am

35

concerned: from almost nothing comes a complete human being.

Early in the winter of 1961 we saw advertised in our local paper a bungalow in Muswell Hill, John's home town, a small pleasant suburb just north of London. Bungalows were very rare in this area and always at a premium. The prospect of the ease of living on one level attracted us both. We made an offer, which to our delight was accepted, and immediately put our maisonette on the market. We sold it to the first couple who saw it, and in the April of that year took possession of the bungalow. It was a typical box-shaped bungalow of no particular attraction. In fact it looked like a child's drawing of a house with the front door in the middle and one window each side, a tall chimney and a small gate with a narrow pathway to the front door. It really was rather like a dolls' house, but the accommodation was just right with one large and one small bedroom, a living room, kitchen and a large extension room on the back which was used as a dining room. French windows from this room led to a lawn with flower beds and at the very end of the garden was a piece of land which had never been cultivated. It was just like a miniature wood with apple trees, fruit bushes and, as we discovered in the spring of that year, masses and masses of bluebells.

The bungalow was centrally heated by a back boiler from the open fire in the living room. We unpacked our belongings, hung new curtains and pictures and very soon it looked like home.

At the ante-natal visit the following week my blood pressure had soared again, so back into hospital I went, back to the boredom of bed-rest and being prodded about. It was late April when I saw the consultant again who informed me that I would have to stay in hospital now until the baby was born. It was not due until 20 May. It seemed like a death sentence to have to stay in that dreary place for at least four weeks and I was really miserable about it. I forgot that John was also suffering at this time. He was lonely and said that the bungalow was just a 'nothing place' without me 'zipping around'. For him too four weeks seemed like seven years. I did not feel quite so sorry for myself after this. I stopped the tears every time he came and resigned myself to make the best of it.

I had plenty of other visitors. My mother came frequently in the afternoons. I felt well but physically very uncomfortable; walking was difficult and my weak spine ached frequently, so most of the time I was confined to bed. The nurses said that they felt happier when I was in bed as it would prevent any risk of falling, as I was so unsteady on my weak leg.

I was in hospital for our first wedding anniversary. Although I did have the red roses, and best wishes from all, I felt cheated at having to celebrate that special first year in hospital. We could not even toast each other in champagne.

Patients were admitted and went to other wards to have their babies and left, and still I remained. I am sure I must have counted every crack in the ceiling of that old building and every mark on the floor tiles a hundred times. If Mark had not arrived by 22 May I was to have a Caesarian section, as the specialist was not happy about my baby getting any bigger than was absolutely necessary, and to quote his words, 'I think you have had enough of lying around'.

On the evening of 20 May I had the most nagging, uncomfortable backache. John had visited me at eight and we sat happily chatting about anything and everything. The sister in charge who had examined me at seven felt sure that the pain low in my spine was the result of pressure on the spinal nerves. 'First babies very rarely come to time, you know,' she said. So I contented myself with this diagnosis and tried to detach myself from this pain. I remember occupying my thoughts by remembering the soprano part of the St Matthew Passion, visualising the entire score and singing quietly to myself. This helped, but a sickening fear kept surfacing through the music in my mind. First, I was afraid that something very wrong was going on inside that had been unnoticed, and secondly that if the pain of giving birth was going to be worse than this then in no way could I stand it.

I then forcibly pulled myself together and pressed the bell above my bed with great determination. A little nurse came into my room. She was certainly younger than me, in fact she hardly looked old enough to be out of school, let alone nursing. She was a tiny red-haired Scot with a freckled face, and confided to me that her name was Joan and that this was, in fact, her first night on duty.

I noticed that it was 11.10 p.m. I explained about the severity of the pain in my lower spine which extended down the inside of my thighs, and said that I wanted to see a doctor.

It so happened that there had been several emergency Caesarians that night so most of the staff, particularly the doctors, were busy. However, Nurse Joan left a message at the operating theatre for a doctor to come down to the ward just as soon as he had finished operating. At 11.40 one of the specialists came to see me. It was the very pleasant Australian who had been looking after me during my entire pregnancy, I can't remember his name now, but the staff always called him Max.

He bustled in with his usual reassuring confidence and asked, 'Well, just how painful is all this then?' I never can understand how one can measure pain. What is bearable to one is unbearable to another. I was taken into an examination room on a trolley, feeling just like a grounded seal, immobile, pain-racked, and so worried that something was wrong. Perhaps the baby was dead and could not be born. Minutes later Max beamed up at me. 'This is terrific,' he said, 'this baby is almost here. You are fully dilated, just one push and we will have him here.' Just twenty minutes later Mark was born, no anaesthetics, no sedatives, just a very speedy normal birth. It was the easiest and most straightforward delivery that anyone could have. I was amazed, and so were all the doctors and nurses who had come to know me so well after all those months.

When the hospital telephoned John shortly after midnight he questioned as to whether there could have been some mistake, as he had only left me at 8.30. Evidently the doctor told him, 'Your wife is very good at all this, you could probably have one a year!' Somehow I don't think that was in the plan.

I really think Mark's birth was one of the happiest times of my life. He was so perfect, all 7 lbs 2 oz of him, those tiny fingers and perfect little feet, and that soft head with just a hint of fair down. Post-natal blues were not for me – I had felt 'blue' enough during the boredom of hospitalisation throughout the pregnancy – for me it was a period of utter maternal contentment and a profound inner peace that all was well.

John was overwhelmed by Mark's arrival. I don't think he had ever believed that the happiness of having a wife and son could be his. The remainder of my hospital stay was enjoyable. I was up and about, receiving good wishes from friends and relatives. My parents were now grandparents, and Gran was a great-grandmother, a real achievement. My in-laws were thrilled to have their first grandson and delighted for both of us. I stayed in hospital for ten days and then we returned to our new home.

John had managed to decorate Mark's small nursery while I had been in hospital. My parents had bought us a pram, John's parents the carry-cot and many extras. Baby clothes in all sizes arrived from John's office staff and many of my aunts who were very good knitters produced some fine knitted coats.

That perfect summer continued, day after day of blue skies and sunshine. Mark was an ideal baby. He slept right through the night within a few weeks and was contented and undemanding (he is still a very undemanding character today). He grew plump and, as he spent all day in the garden, became as brown as a berry. He had a naturally sunny disposition and was known locally as 'Merry Mark' as he beamed enthusiastically at everyone.

There were very few physical problems to cope with when he was a small baby, but as he grew big and heavy and started to crawl at great speed at the age of nine months, he was very difficult for me to lift. This I resolved by leaving a cloth harness on him at all times. I could then bend down, supporting myself on one side by holding on to a piece of furniture, and hoist him up with the other hand. We suspended a baby-bouncer in the kitchen doorway and this he absolutely loved. My mother and mother-in-law took it in turns to take him for long walks in the afternoon while I got on with any chores or had a rest.

That year was a memorable one. My brother Tony passed his driving test on the day of Mark's birth, and three weeks later my sister-in-law Betty gave birth also to a son, Gareth, so there was a cousin for Mark. John went into partnership with a friend of his. It had always been his ambition to have a professional practice specialising in commercial taxation, a chance for him to use all his expertise and experience. John's offices were in north London, just twenty minutes away from our home. The practice grew rapidly and within three months John and his partner were needing some help in the office, so it was arranged that I should do a couple of mornings secretarial work each week. Meanwhile the grandmas took it in turns to come and look after Mark, who accepted the arrangement quite happily.

By the time Mark had his first birthday, he was a very large sturdy boy who walked well and was the proud possessor of four teeth. With his almost white hair and tanned body he looked very Swedish. He had not had a day's illness in his first year, and I can't remember ever having a disturbed night.

I began taking part again in the musical world that I loved, singing in a few concerts, and had the odd singing lesson here and there. Music for me is 'food for my soul' and still plays a vital part in my life today.

Our standard of living was good, and one of my dreams came true when John arranged for us to share regularly a box at Covent Garden with another couple. We experienced some wonderful times there. We both had a love of music, enjoyed opera, ballet, concerts and live theatre. I could lose myself in my fantasy world.

John and I still were very involved with the British Polio Fellowship. He played an active part as Secretary and we used to attend the monthly meetings, taking Mark with us. Mark became a popular member, thoroughly spoilt by all, and used to keep the members entertained with his antics, particularly climbing. He would climb up on anything in sight, chairs, tables, the piano – we could never take our eyes off him for a minute.

Those first two years of marriage were perfect: John's business doing well and our home full of so much love, tenderness and laughter and the ultimate joy we both experienced in our little son. The thrills of finding those first pearly teeth, watching his first steps, hearing his first word were all so exciting, particularly special because it was the first time.

7 A little princess

In July 1962 I became pregnant again. I was pleased but dreaded the prospect of any further troubles with blood pressure which would take me into hospital for weeks at a time. Having to leave Mark would have been unbearable.

The two grandmas came to the rescue again, and I rested every afternoon for two hours, kept on a very low-calorie, salt-free diet which seemed to do the trick, and I had very little trouble at all, apart from the obvious problem of mobility in the late stages of pregnancy. We were both so lucky to have the support of our parents. My mother in particular went out of her way to do all she could to make this pregnancy as trouble-free as possible.

The winter was extremely severe that year. From Boxing Day until early April thick snow lay everywhere and the temperature never lifted. I was housebound, as I never have been able to keep my balance in the snow and have had many painful falls. The only time I went out was at weekends when John had the car. Mark used to get fed up with having to stay in so much and it was quite a dreary time for us both as the weeks dragged by.

My own local GP specialised in obstetrics and I went to see him to try to persuade him to let me have this baby at home, mainly on the grounds that the previous birth had been so straightforward and rapid. He agreed on the understanding that if the slightest problem arose he would send me into hospital.

Clare was born on 20 March 1963 on a very cold night. There had been a fresh fall of snow that week. My doctor stayed the whole night with me, just to make sure that everything went well. Everything was just as straightforward as before, only this time I was aware of what those severe back pains were. Previously I had not connected them with being in labour.

Clare was as pretty as a picture from the word go and John christened her his little princess. She certainly had beautiful features, a tiny nose and rosebud mouth and very large eyes that changed from blue to green in her first year. But she was not the model baby that her brother had been, which was rather a shock. She seemed to suffer constant throat and chest infections and wheezed and coughed most nights.

The doctor said that she caught frequent colds which went straight to her chest. I am convinced now that she suffered a severe allergy to cow's milk but as little or nothing was accepted about allergy then, I continued to give her the very substance which must have been like pumping poison into her. She was on almost continuous antibiotics which helped for a short time, but was very restless by day and at night cried a lot and had problems with her breathing. Had she been the first baby I doubt if there would have been any more!

The relaxed, happy time we had in Mark's babyhood was certainly not repeated, for even when she was free from infections she was unhappy and irritable a lot of the time.

I took her backwards and forwards to our local doctor and clinic, until they got sick of seeing me. I became labelled as an 'over-anxious mother', yet I still had this gut feeling that something somewhere was wrong. However, she grew into another strapping child with the bonus of a head of most glorious curls, as befitted a little princess.

I became very irritable and tired mainly because of lack of sleep. On one occasion after a bout of bronchitis when I had not been to bed for two nights my mother came to the rescue and took Clare home with her. I think I slept for about 18 hours!

John's prophecy was that things could not remain as they were, she must improve. We had had all sorts of tests and X-rays and nothing abnormal had been discovered apart from her chest condition, which I suppose if the doctors had been honest would have been diagnosed as 'bronchial asthma'.

John's spinal deformity used to have an effect on his breathing upon exertion, and it was at this time that his condition started to worsen. He was constantly tired and often after a day's work at the office would come home exhausted and breathless and go straight to sleep for hours. He also found it hard to concentrate on his work which caused him tremendous anxiety. He did visit a doctor but he could find no real cause for the deterioration in John's health.

I suppose I felt very lonely at this time, almost in fact as if I was alone on an island. The children tired John even more. A feeling of gloom descended over everybody and everything. I am sure that when one gets caught up in this negative atmosphere it invites just more doom and gloom into your life. It is almost like a fly caught up in a spider's web, the more he struggles and wriggles the tighter he embeds himself in the web. We were all in this sticky entangled web of illness which casts a negative spell over any environment.

I don't think I ever appreciated the extent of John's suffering at that time. He was far too tired most of the time to want to go anywhere or do anything much apart from his job, while I wanted more outside interests, more social life. I was only 24 and all this was just too much, too soon.

John was so passionately proud of his children and I would catch him bending over their cots when they were asleep and tears would roll uncontrollably down his cheeks. 'I have my Lady Precious Stream,' he would say, 'you were the best thing that ever happened to me, and now I have my two children. Clare is your double, so even when you are 60 I will be able to remember you at 20 by just looking at her.'

I often question what this love is, the love a mother has for her child even in its unborn stage. It is not only a feeling of tremendous protection, defence and caring, children actually are a part of you, you carry them close to your heart and there they always remain, whether they are five years old or 50.

The love between a man and woman is quite different. They are not a part of each other, there is no blood relationship, so to be right it must be the communion of two souls. It is not enough just to love in the physical sense – that fades – it must also be the tuning-in of two minds. It means true friendship, and you should be able to say anything to a friend, confide your innermost thoughts, fears, weaknesses, and inhibitions.

I am a great believer in laughter: laugh at your stupidities, your petty disagreements. The greatest destroyer of any relationship is silence. It is lethal, and any partnership, be it marriage, business, parent and child, where one or other person retreats into 'the thunder of silence' over any disagreement or upset will build up such tremendous tension that it will eventually shatter into a thousand pieces. I prefer to 'explode' when I am angry and then return to normal within minutes when peace can be restored.

It was because we had both suffered the frustration of disability, the loneliness that goes with separation from family at a tender age, the pain attached to a long illness, and the very real fight to get back into living with normal able-bodied people and make something of our lives that John and I felt we shared a common bond. John's positive attitude to life, strength of character and uncomplaining nature were qualities which I respected and admired. He taught me a lot, he had a fine brain and a wide knowledge of many subjects. He had studied the lives of great poets, artists and musicians and had the same passionate love of music, especially the classics.

In March 1964, Clare had her first birthday. She was such a picture with those enormous green appealing eyes and tight corn-coloured ringlets, that wherever I went I was stopped by endless admirers. Her chest condition seemed to improve in the summer months, but she still had periods of irritability for which I could never find a reason. She made no attempt to crawl, seeming content to sit on the floor.

We went on holiday that May, renting a small cottage in Cornwall, and it seemed to have a rejuvenating effect upon us all. John's health had improved, he was less tired, his breathing was back to normal as it had been before the downward trend of the previous six months.

So we returned to some good days, free days, with lots of love and laughter. The practice was still expanding and we enjoyed a good standard of living. Mark was now a fine, strong boy of three who had just started at a morning playgroup which he thoroughly enjoyed. I still worked two mornings per week, enjoying the change of scene and feeling that in some small way I helped to stimulate the business and support John.

I decided to apply to the Ministry of Health for a hand-controlled Invacar – they used to be issued to disabled people quite freely, and as our car was used by John every day, having my own transport would give me the opportunity to expand and develop the quality of my life. I filled in endless forms, went up to London for a medical, had an interview with one of the officials – and within a comparatively short time my pale blue Invacar arrived. Mark instantly christened it 'Pop' as it made a loud popping noise, particularly when one started up the engine which made a noise like a motor-bike.

After some very basic driving instruction from a Ministry of Health instructor I started to enjoy my new freedom. Now I would be able to visit friends, go shopping alone, and visit my mother in the afternoons. It really was bliss. From that day the children and I had a new-found freedom which improved our life in many directions.

Clare was still not walking. Every attempt to stand caused an instant collapse on the floor and she seemed quite unable to keep her balance which caused her intense frustration.

My intuition that all was not well with her proved right. One afternoon while we were in the garden, I noticed that the new cotton trousers she was wearing seemed to show a difference in the length of the legs. Clare was holding on like grim death to the edge of a deck chair to keep from falling. I remember that terrible sensation in my stomach as I removed her trousers, measured them and found that the trouser legs were identical; it was her legs that were not. Frantically I stripped off all her clothes and laid her on the grass. Both legs seemed identical, but on standing her up again I could see that the left hip went right up into the socket when she stood, and consequently her knees were not level.

I experienced a mass of instant mixed emotions: anger at the stupidity of the clinic doctor who had seen and examined her and her legs and hips so many times in the past year and had called me 'an over-anxious mother'; fear as to what actually was wrong and how serious it was; and guilt at having been so short-tempered with her.

I quickly dressed Clare, and got on the telephone to my doctor and insisted on an appointment. I remember the receptionist saying, 'We are heavily booked up today.' 'I'll wait until the end of the afternoon,' I said, 'but I insist on being seen today.'

The doctor confirmed my fears later that afternoon when he found that Clare had a congenital dislocation of the left hip which would need extensive treatment to rectify. It did not help when he said that this condition could have been quickly put right if it had been discovered at birth as he was the one who had delivered her! The pieces all fitted neatly into the jigsaw now and explained why she cried when I changed her nappy or if the push-chair bumped down a kerb, and why she could not get her balance. Within a week Clare was admitted into Great Ormond Street Hospital.

The emotion you experience when you have to allow a strong, healthy 18-month-old to lie on her back for weeks in traction is indescribable. In fact it is torture. John and I shed many tears these next few weeks. We felt as if our world had come to an end. Clare must have felt very rejected and lonely.

I visited Clare daily. Up into London I went in 'Pop'. Surely the good Lord must have known what was ahead, as without transport there was no way I would have been able to visit her daily.

We were amazed at how Clare accepted her immobility, but she did, and even seemed to have an 'inner peace' that was never there before. She seemed to understand that what was being done was for her benefit. She was content, even though her legs and hips were pulled at straight angles above her head. Every few days her legs were pulled apart a few inches, the object being that at the end of the six-week treatment, the traction would have put the bone at the top of the thigh back into the socket. Then either it would have to be pinned into place by surgery, or she would go into a frog plaster for a long period.

There were wards full of babies suffering from severe congenital deformities, brain tumours, blood diseases and leukaemia.

I remember during visiting one day seeing a little girl of about seven or eight years of age struggle towards me with two calipers, a spinal jacket, supporting herself on two elbow crutches. She had a great big brave smile and, seeing that I too had a caliper and a stick, asked, 'When do you think I will be able to walk as well as you?' My arms went instantly round her and my tears were uncontrollable as I knew from the nurses on the ward that she had spinal cancer and had only a short time to live.

Another little boy walked on his new artificial leg. He was so confident and positive about life – I chatted away quite merrily with him. I learned that he had lost his leg in a car crash in which both his parents were killed. He was only 11, but somehow he had managed to overcome losing a leg and losing his parents too. 'I'm going back to live with me Nan,' he said, 'and I want to try football again.' My mind instantly flashed back to Charlie in Coxen Ward when I was ten and he eight: the wheelchair races, the efforts to walk between parallel bars, the falls, the tears and smiles, my first love.

I do believe in the hereafter, I do believe that life is governed by immutable laws of cause and effect and that what you give out of yourself is returned to you. If you give love you must receive it; if you hate, then you will be hated; if you are negative and gloomy then you will invite these elements into your life. We must face life with courage, however hard or painful it must be, but never, never will I understand how tiny innocent babies are destined to suffer when they have not even experienced living, and I question God, or perhaps it should be Man, when I see young children having to go through such intense pain and suffering.

I read in a book recently that we experience sickness or deformity as a result of pain and suffering we caused to others in previous lives. Who knows?

The nursing staff at Great Ormond Street were incredibly caring, and they must have always carried the sound of children's voices in their ears whether they were on duty or not. We felt very humble and our daughter's problem became a very small one when we realised that in time it could be totally rectified.

During the months of visiting Clare in hospital I felt increasingly that I should be working in the field of healing, preferably with children. Though nursing would be out of the question as it was physically too demanding, I still felt that I had a lot to offer.

The summer passed. Clare had progressed from traction and was put into a 'frog plaster'. She was totally encased in heavy plaster from just below her armpits to both ankles and was fixed with her legs at right angles, just like a frog. At this stage of her treatment she should have been transferred to the country branch of Great Ormond Street Hospital in Tadworth, Surrey, but I fought against this as visiting would have been so restrictive. The hospital staff were very helpful and arranged to transfer Clare to the children's ward of a local general hospital in Winchmore Hill, near to where we lived.

The sister in charge was a friendly efficient Scot, and Clare very soon became 'her baby' and the favourite. A large old pram was found and I was able to take her out into the acres of ground in which this hospital had been built. Sister really did all she could to help us, and I shall always be eternally grateful to her for her humanity. She had a special little seat constructed for Clare by the hospital carpenter. It was just like a horse's saddle with a little back to it, so Clare could sit astride. We were allowed to visit her whenever we wished and together we all struggled through those difficult months. X-rays revealed that Clare's hip was actually moulding back into the badly formed socket. Every two months she was taken back to Great Ormond Street by ambulance for the plaster to be removed and a larger one fitted.

Clare was two years and three months old when the monstrous plaster was removed. I shall never forget the little stick-like wasted legs and the hip-bones that protruded through the skin. She was immediately placed into a leather and metal frame from waist to knees which still kept her in the frog position, so that all she could do was to scurry about on the floor just like a little frog.

She was very heavy and awkward for us to cope with physically. It brought many extra problems for us both, but as always our parents rallied round and helped in every way they could. Meanwhile Mark started full-time school. I often felt that he had taken a back seat during this period, but it could not be helped.

8 A sad parting

They say that troubles never come singly, and they certainly did not for us. Clare started to walk by the time she was three, with a staggering gait rather like a drunken sailor. We bought her a truck on wheels to push along, and this seemed to give her that extra confidence that she lacked. Within a few months she was walking normally, a great success thanks to modern technology.

It was almost as if, just as Clare became well, John became ill. In fact this was not really true; it was just that during the months when I was wrapped up with visiting her – all my spare time was lavished upon her, up and down to Great Ormond Street in 'Pop' (thank goodness the traffic was not as congested as it is today) – I did not notice how ill and weak John had become. Friends and relatives had noticed the deterioration but I was blind, blind because my thoughts had been concentrated upon Clare.

John was now having difficulty coping with his job. Evidently his partner had been complaining that there were errors in his work, and complaints had been voiced by many clients. Our doctor could find no real cause for his symptoms, and thought that perhaps the pressure of his job was proving just too much for him. He wondered if a consultation with a psychiatrist might help, particularly as his forgetfulness and declining standard of work pointed to some sort of nervous disorder. This was all a waste of time and I knew that the doctors were 'barking up the wrong tree'. John no more needed a psychiatrist than I did. No doubt Clare's problems had caused extra strain, but I was sure that this was not the cause.

His mental abilities were deteriorating rapidly. It was pathetic to watch a man who had been blessed with such a fine brain struggle to add up a column of figures. It was a terrible blow to his ego and an insult to his intelligence to have to step down from his partnership and take a far lesser job in a firm of accountants in the City. He suffered a great deal over this and became frustrated at the constant bouts of lethargy that he had to fight.

Our lifestyle had to change, since we were now on a much lower income. We talked over our problems and decided to move out of London to a country environment where property was much cheaper, there was less stress and strain, and there would be a healthier environment for our children to grow up in. John already had a small part-time private practice which he worked on during the weekends. He was sure that he could expand this by advertising and then find employment in a much lesser capacity in a neighbouring town.

We started looking for property within about 30 miles of London and found a development of new bungalows in a small village just 30 miles north of London. It was Hatfield Broad Oak, in Essex. It was such a pretty village when we first visited it in August 1966. Situated at the top of a steep hill surrounded by miles and miles of country, it had an old pub in the centre, a small sub-Post Office which was the gathering place of the whole community, two further pubs on the outskirts of the village with beams and brasses everywhere and enormous fireplaces, and an old-fashioned bakery with a real brick oven from which the most delicious smells pervaded the whole village square daily. There was a very ancient pump in the village square. The old coach house had been converted and extended into a more modern development.

The houses were individual: thatched cottages or old slate-roofed terrace cottages with a front door that opened straight into a small living room. There was a small, friendly village school on one side of the main road opposite the most enormous church, almost like a cathedral, which seemed quite out of place in such a small environment. The school was a hub of activity and a meeting-place for all mothers and children. There were no more than 20 children in any one class and the atmosphere was very personal.

I felt that this spot was the right one for us. The bungalows, only twelve in all, were in a small cul-de-sac. Each property was detached in a reasonable piece of land, with three bedrooms, a large living room, large kitchen-diner, bathroom and toilet and separate cloakroom – all for £4,800. We decided to buy Lucas Cottage – evidently the farmer who owned the land on which the bungalows had been built was a Mr Lucas – with the plan that John would stay on with his job in London for a couple of months until he could find another or see if he could develop his own private practice.

He seemed happy about leaving London. His health and confidence took a turn for the better and he was holding down this job quite well. We sold our London bungalow very quickly, and moved on 2 December 1966. It was a freezing day and the wind whipped around that little village as we worked hard to get ourselves ship-shape. There was no decorating to do this time as the bungalow was new and everywhere was emulsioned in attractive pastel shades. The kitchen was fully fitted, but there was no central heating and it was so terribly cold having been empty for several months. We did eventually light a fire in the living room, but birds had taken a fancy to nesting in the chimney and we were almost smoked out that first evening. We had to forget the fire and manage with a couple of electric fires until we found a local chimney sweep. The garden needed laying out, but that would have to wait until the spring.

What a contrast to London! There were no street lights and in some places no real pavements, and of course we did not know anybody.

Mark soon settled down in his new school environment. He thought it was great fun to be able to ride to school on his bike without any worry about traffic, and Clare was going to be allowed to start at Easter when she was four.

The greatest worry about the move as far as she was concerned was the fact that all her clothes were not hanging in a wardrobe. She had a passion for clothes which was overwhelming. Even at four she was terribly clothes-conscious and adored the feel of fabrics. Her greatest thrill was a pair of black patent leather shoes, which she called her 'pavement shoes'. She insisted on sleeping with them on for several nights. There was my sleeping angel in her pink frilly nightdress and two black patent shoes sticking out of the end of the bed. The most important decision every evening was what she was going to wear the following day.

Her enthusiasm for clothes, however, was very wearing when she used to wake me up at 5 in the morning to tie her blonde curls into ribbons; the ribbons had to match the colour of the clothes that she was to wear that day. She did eventually become more civilised about her waking hours, but it took a long time. She is still obsessive about her clothes and as fussy as ever about matching tones of colours. However, her colour sense is wonderful and she also has a flair for interior design.

Our new-found security and happiness was so short-lived, almost like a small patch of blue sky on a cloudy day when there is just a faint hope of a good day ahead. All too soon, however, the sky clouds over and everything is grey and dull. It was just like that for us, a hint of blue and then a build-up of heavy clouds. John was taken ill the following Saturday morning, just one week after we had moved in. He had tremendous difficulty in breathing, his face was grey and his eyes sunken.

I found the local doctor and called him in. Obviously he knew nothing of John's past history, had no notes, nothing to go by, but he was worried that there seemed to be some bronchial pneumonia in both lungs. John was instantly put on antibiotics but later that day he seemed worse, so again I went down to the surgery and asked the doctor to call.

He came back with me immediately and decided to admit John to hospital.

I had to stay behind. There was no way I could travel with him as I had the children and it was very late at night. John was his usual positive self – it was just another knock, another blow to contend with. He had no idea of the severity of his condition, but I knew, I knew by his laboured breathing and weakness and by the expression of the doctor. As I watched the ambulance go down the drive, I knew that he was not going to be with us for very long. He would never see his lovely children grow up and I would have to go through the rest of my life without him.

It was cold and so lonely in that bungalow and I was afraid. I wished that we had never moved away from our families. I had no telephone, as it had not yet been connected, and we had not even finished unpacking. Boxes of books, china and pictures and a great chest full of the children's toys filled the third bedroom, and it was difficult to know where to start.

The following day was Sunday and I wanted to visit the hospital although I dreaded it, dreaded hearing the worst, was frightened to hear the truth. I was annoyed at myself for being so pessimistic. The doctor had arranged with a local lady to sit with the children while I visited the hospital. It was in Chelmsford, only 16 miles away but it seemed much further. We now had a Morris 1000, especially hand-controlled for me, so 'Pop' had gone from my life.

I found the Chelmsford and Essex Hospital, was directed to the ward and could hardly believe my eyes when I found John looking terribly weak and pale in an oxygen tent. He gave me a smile, asked after the children and then faded off into a coma-like sleep. I could hardly believe the change in him. Just 24 hours previously he had been chatting away happily, treating his condition as just a case of pneumonia. I sat for the remainder of that hour in a daze, wondering if this were all a bad dream, until my thoughts were interrupted by a doctor who beckoned me into his office. I knew exactly what he was going to say.

'Your husband has only a short time to live. I am afraid there has been massive internal damage to his lungs owing to the major operations he had on his spine as a young boy. He is living on about a quarter of the average oxygen capacity, it amazes us how he has kept going for as long as he has. This is the reason he has been suffering from lack of concentration and has been unable to do his job – lack of oxygen to his brain.

'We are not sure, we think he may recover from this attack but he will be very much of an invalid, unable of course to work and I doubt if he will survive for more than another two or three years.

'We are sorry, we are doing everything possible, but we felt you must know the truth.'

Then I seemed to be surrounded by people: a nurse, a social worker, and many kind things were said: 'It's so hard for a young woman like you with young children, but it's best to keep going for their sake.' I did not take it all in, could only think of the cruelty of life to rob a man of such a good brain and such strength of character, to be stuck like a cabbage in a field, a useless invalid. He was such a proud man that a life like that would be a torture.

My tears flowed, tears of sadness, and frustration, for there was nothing that anybody could do. Eventually a nurse came in with some tea and kindly offered me a bed at the hospital for the night, but I had to get back, back to my children who were going to need me now more than ever.

I went out into that dark murky night, back to the car, to our new bungalow. It was still snowing, and as I drove home I thought of all the plans we had made together, the things we intended to do, places we meant to visit, his hopes and wishes for the children, all just wasted and futile now. Then there were the practical issues: how and on what we were going to live if John were going to be a permanent invalid? I knew that without his work, without being able to read, study and use his brain he would not wish to live.

I don't remember the drive home. Somehow by some miracle I got back, thanked the babysitter, looked in on my sleeping children, and vowed that whatever happened they were going to have every possible opportunity. God only knew how I would do it, but somehow I would.

The telephone was connected the following day, so at least I now had some instant contact with the outside world. My parents arrived to give me some moral support and daily I visited the hospital.

John did improve after he was put on powerful steroids through a drip infusion in his arm. His breathing improved, and within a week he was able to sit in a chair and regain his bright cheerful disposition. His usual positive attitude returned, he talked about returning to work, about the children and treated his illness as something very uncomplicated.

Christmas came. John had a very bad relapse on Christmas Eve, and did not feel well enough to have visitors. I took the children just for a few minutes on Christmas morning. They ran up to him with their presents, but he was far too ill to join in with the celebrations. The nurses had decorated the ward so beautifully, there was an enormous Christmas tree at the end of it, and yet I knew that the man in the corner would not be able to enjoy this Christmas and that he would never see another one.

John remained in hospital until the end of January when he seemed a lot better, was able to walk about and wanted to come home. He returned to us in February. An oxygen cylinder was supplied in case of breathing difficulties and the doctor came in once and often twice a day. Although the pneumonia had cleared, John was still a very sick man and spent most of his time in a chair in a deep sleep. Every day was a nightmare, and every night was even worse as he frequently had to have oxygen throughout the night and at every move, every turn, I was awake, helping him with the oxygen mask.

If there is a God, I prayed, please let him die, don't let him live in this terrible state any longer, release him from all this suffering.

Every day I went about like a robot, getting the children's breakfast, taking them to school. Clare had been allowed to start a term earlier, mainly to get her away from all the problems at home.

In the children's eyes, the problems were minuscule. People fell ill and became well again. They were far too young to realise the severity of their father's condition. They still came home to a supposedly normal mother who provided a comfortable home and all the love and affection that was theirs as a right.

One evening when John's breathing was so laboured that I really felt he must be dying, I got the children up out of their beds, bundled them into the car and off we went to the hospital. An injection helped ease the situation and we came back again. Not only do you have to fight the constant welling up of emotion as you daily watch such suffering, but you have to fight to create an atmosphere as detached as possible from fear, for your children.

Early in March the deep coma-like states increased and it became impossible to cope any longer, so John was re-admitted into hospital. At the same time, I began to feel unwell myself, and I had strong suspicions that I might be pregnant. I went to my doctor who felt sure that my condition had resulted from the months of stress and worry which had completely upset my whole system. I accepted this diagnosis, but still had a strong feeling that he was wrong.

Back I went to the daily visits to hospital, to watch all the pain and suffering which I knew was to no avail. John was attached to a steroid drip in one arm, a drip in the other to save him from dehydration, and had been put back into an oxygen tent.

'Why do you let him go through all this suffering when you know he is going to die?' I asked the doctors. 'Would it not be kinder to turn off the drips, turn off the oxygen and leave him?'

'We do have to try to support life. I'm sorry, we are doing out best.'

I realised at this time that it was my responsibility to talk to Mark and Clare about death, something they knew nothing about. I explained that everybody had to die, animals and birds as well, but that our spirit, which was the happy part of us, went on living for ever and that all we left behind was a worn-out shell. When people died we did not see them again until we ourselves were old and worn-out and then we met them in heaven.

'If the doctors cannot make Daddy well, he will die as well, but it will be much better for him to die and for his spirit to go to heaven than to have to suffer not being able to breathe any longer. Daddy does not want to live like this and I don't want him to suffer any longer than is possible.'

'Do you wear pyjamas in heaven?' Mark asked. 'Do you sleep in bed, and do you get very wet if it rains if you are living in the clouds?' asked Clare. 'Will Daddy be able to see us when he is in heaven?'

I answered their questions as simply and as honestly as I could, but it was hard to find the right words to satisfy them.

In mid-March I went back to ask for a pregnancy test. Just a few days later it was confirmed that I was in fact three months pregnant.

I suppose I really should have become hysterical and frantic. My doctor was very worried about my mental and physical health and offered me the choice of an abortion if I so wished. In any event he would arrange an appointment for me to see a friend of his, a gynaecologist, a super man, he said, just as soon as possible. In the meantime he would leave it to me to decide what was the best thing to do.

In some uncanny way I knew that this pregnancy was meant to be, although I could not think why or how I was going to cope with another child on my own. My parents were so worried, but I think my mother shared my feeling that there was no way I could part with this little life. I would hang on to this little boy like grim death as I knew he would be just a duplicate of his father, whom in any case I was going to lose. There was just no purpose in losing both of them. Abortion would be the easy way out, but it was not for me.

I visited the gynaecologist the following week. He was a very human, friendly man, who understood exactly my feelings. 'Be guided by your instincts,' he said, and so I was.

Would it be best to tell John about this baby, I wondered, would it give him some pleasure to know that despite all this illness we had produced something 'special' together? Although the baby was obviously never planned, maybe the news would give John a lift of spirits.

Clare had her fourth birthday on 20 March. We celebrated it as best as we could and when I visited John that evening I told him about the birthday presents, her party, the cake, and then I added, 'How would you feel if I told you that we are going to have another baby?'

'Delighted,' he said, 'provided you are, he's turned up at quite the wrong time.'

'Who said anything about "he"?' I said.

'This one is going to be just like me, that I know – with brown eyes and dark hair, no more blonds with green eyes.'

You are right, I thought, 'just like you', a strong continuation of you. What a shame you will never see him.

That was the last time I ever spoke to John. The next few days brought intensive suffering, as the strong drugs he was given made his poor body flinch and twist about, but still he never complained. I would stroke his forehead, hold his hand and watch the pain in those lovely dark brown twinkling eyes, which had now become dull and pain-racked.

He seemed to accept his suffering without question, and all he ever said was how he was going to get well and live with his 'Lady Precious Stream' and his lovely children. Constantly he told me how he loved and needed me and valued every minute of his life with me.

Just 24 hours later John went into a coma, and on 22 March 1967 he was released from all his suffering. I was content that he had died happy in the knowledge that he had left behind a tiny speck of humanity, an extension of himself.

9 And then we were four

I had no more tears to shed. The supply had been utterly exhausted in the preceding months. In a way I felt as if a burden had been lifted: a relief that I did not have to sit and watch John suffering any longer, frustrated that there was nothing I could do to help, except to be there. Life is only of value when there is quality. John's life did not possess it.

My brother-in-law Gwyn came down from Nottingham the following morning to sort out all the miserable legalities connected with death, and I had to go back to the hospital that day to be handed back one black sack of John's belongings, a gold wedding ring, a gold watch, a photograph of me which he insisted on having on his locker at all times, some pyjamas and a dressing gown. At home there were his clothes and personal belongings. I found some old diaries of his and turned to the page which mentioned that he had met 'Ann; she is only 18, but gives out so much love and warmth that I really think I love her, I wonder if she will feel that I am too old for her'.

You cannot believe as you step into the outside world again, out of the hospital that offered only hope but not a miracle – and that was what he needed – that life goes on just as usual. Surely the world should have ended with his death. It was such an immense tragedy – he was so unique and special in my life. It was a wet misty March morning, no different from any other March morning. The usual routines of life were relentlessly going on: people queuing for buses, people driving to work, traffic jams, milk floats, the postman delivering letters as usual. Everything was going on just as before, and it always would for we were just microscopic specks of humanity in the vastness of the universe and the same principles of life would continue forever. Cause and effect, life and death – there would never be any change in that pattern.

I didn't want flowers for his funeral – flowers are for the living. I still have very strong views on flowers at funerals. It is the spirit of the person we love, not just the physical body which at the end of life is just discarded, rather like a cardboard box housing a beautiful oil painting. Instead of flowers I requested that donations be made to the British Polio Fellowship, and quite a large sum of money was collected for the respiratory unit.

After the funeral, about which I remember very little, I went back to London with the children to be with my parents for some moral support. I felt I needed somebody to look after me, and no one was better than my mother at that. I returned home in April. The children were flourishing, they had accepted that Daddy had gone to heaven as I had predicted and that he really was happy now and able to breathe and there was no more suffering. Clare and Mark loved village life. They had such freedom, were able to ride their bikes around the village without any fear of being run over, and the school was excellent, far superior to the town school they would have gone to in London.

However, I hated the place, wished that we had never left London, longed to be near my parents and friends and relatives, wanted to return to the comfort of familiarity, like traffic and street lights and shops, things that I had said I would be happy to leave. I vowed I would return. Next year I would go back, after my son was born.

Our financial situation was quite good, and although it seems dreadful to have to think, so soon after a death, of things like how bills are to be paid these things do have to be sorted out and as soon as possible. The mortgage had been paid off by an insurance policy, I had a pension from the Chartered Accountants' Benevolent Association and the state pension, which meant that ends did actually meet each month. Money is not everything, it does not bring back people who are dear to you, but it certainly helps to soften the blow.

April passed into May, May to June, and the Essex countryside was just so beautiful, acres and acres of undulating countryside, wonderful trees, thatched cottages, beautiful period homes standing in equally delightful gardens. It was all so peaceful and so different from London with its grim grey terraces of houses and hardly a tree in sight, main roads bustling with streams of traffic, exhaust fumes and crowds and crowds of people. Village life had started to grow on me. Here I was one of a small group, people seemed to care about each other, my children had found a new freedom and a better life than would have been possible in London.

'We must go back to London next year,' I said.

'I wish we could live here for ever,' said Mark. 'We don't want to go back there, we have made lots of friends.'

Weekdays were reasonably easy to cope with but evenings were lonely after my children were in bed at seven. Although I had obviously had to get rid of all John's clothes, I had kept back a very special tweed sports coat which was my favourite. It smelt like him and when I was lonely in the evenings I used to sit wearing it. The feel and smell of familiarity – that's what the jacket meant to me, and I was not ashamed of my need. It was a comfort, rather like a favourite old piece of cloth that a child clings to at night.

My mother's brother George came to visit me shortly after John's death. He was a writer, in fact he was the editor of a newspaper.'Why don't you write about your life in these last 28 years?' he suggested. 'So much has happened to you, it would make such good reading, and I think it would help you emotionally to put all your feelings, experiences, hurts, pains and partings down on to paper. I will give you all the help I can.'

So in the evenings I put on John's old jacket and got out John's old typewriter. I had bought a large supply of typing paper and as soon as my little ones were settled for the night, I started to write. At the same time I got out all my favourite music, Beethoven, Mozart, Verdi, Strauss, on went the music and I started typing. I could not leave 'my story' alone. It helped me immensely and was a wonderful therapy. I decided to call it 'Climb Every Mountain', and it would be completed by the birth of my son. Eventually I was to sell my story to *Woman's Own*. 'Climb Every Mountain' was serialised in two parts and brought an enormous amount of interest from the public. One day, I thought, when I am older, I will write the sequel to this, and that is what I am doing now.

However sad or unhappy you are, life does go on. Regardless of whatever tragedy may befall, every morning the sun rises and every evening we can be sure of it setting. The seasons come and go century after century. Despite all the grief, wars and suffering, life continues, and so did mine.

In those early months of us being alone I used to read book after book to the children before they went to bed, but what they liked best were my 'head stories' – stories that I made up for them. 'Sit down and tell us a head story,' they would say, and so I would start.

'There was a beautiful Princess, who was you, Clare, and a handsome Prince, who was you, Mark. The Princess lived in a wonderful castle on the top of a hill. The castle was surrounded by a moat and within the castle grounds were the most wonderful peacocks you ever did see with their magnificent feathers, which were all the colours of the rainbow.

'The Princess was terribly lonely and unhappy. She was never allowed out of the castle grounds, so really she was a prisoner. Her father was a fearsome King who was most possessive about his beautiful daughter and was determined that nobody would marry her.

'The Princess used to climb to the highest tower in the castle and with a telescope watch the Prince ride by every day on his black stallion which was the swiftest horse in the kingdom. The Prince had heard so much about the Princess and desperately wanted to get into the castle and save her from her lonely life. Unknown to the King the Prince was able to put people into a trance merely by lifting his right arm and pointing in the direction of the person he wanted to put into a trance-like sleep. One evening the Prince approached the castle with the request that he had an urgent message for the King. The drawbridge was let down and as he approached the castle door he lifted his arm and pointed his finger at each of the guards who immediately fell into a deep deep sleep. As he ran through the castle he cast his magic spell upon everyone he came into contact with, even the miserable old King. The Prince climbed until he reached the Princess in the highest tower and fled away with her on his black stallion. They rode away to another country, far far away from the King and the unhappy life that the Princess had experienced in the castle.

'Eventually the Prince and Princess reached a beautiful land, married and had lots and lots of lovely children.'

'Did the Prince die and go to heaven?' asked Mark.

'No, dear, he did not die until he was very old and worn out and then they both died and went to heaven together.'

'Head stories' were a firm favourite for many years, and even when they reached eight and nine were a special treat. Eventually I ran out of ideas; we had had stories about rabbits and foxes, families of mice trying to escape from the clutches of the family cat, mermaids and mermen, gnomes and witches, dragons and brave warriors, and my children never tired of them.

In some mysterious way I was detached from my advancing pregnancy, and at times I felt as if I was almost standing outside myself, looking in at somebody else going through this experience. I could not imagine actually having another baby to rear on my own, could not imagine four of us living in that bungalow, and so I made absolutely no preparations for his arrival, no feverish knitting, no window-gazing for baby equipment, nor did I want anybody else to make things for him either. My pram and baby equipment had been parted with a couple of years previously as we had only intended a family of two.

Every time I went to the ante-natal clinic I waited for the doctor to say, 'Sorry, there is no heartbeat, your baby is dead'. I was constantly anticipating a miscarriage. I took no care of my health whatsoever, ate a lot of rubbish, took no vitamins or supplements, simply because I could not identify myself with the situation, could not believe that I was pregnant, that I would have a baby in a few months. It was this 'other woman' who was going through all this, not me.

In July my blood pressure decided to soar and my mother came for a couple of weeks as I had to spend most of the day in bed. Then an old aunt moved in with me until I was admitted to hospital in the middle of August for labour to be induced. Clare went to stay with a cousin of mine in Barnet, and Mark went to stay with my parents in London.

The Irish sister in the Maternity Unit in Chelmsford was sensitive enough to decide to put me into a small side ward with two unmarried mothers. At least that would spare me the heartache of watching other fathers visit their wives and babies.

I really cannot remember anything about Jonathan's birth. It is still a complete blur, almost as if a large slate had been rubbed clean of all information. I cannot remember the induction, have no recollection of any pain and do not recall the overwhelming experience of emotion at birth. I still felt as if I was standing outside myself, looking in at another woman going through this experience. I remember feeling so sorry for this woman, desperately wanted to comfort her, hold her hand and give her the strength to face the future. On another occasion I felt as if I was stepping into her mind, sharing the suffering, taking the responsibility for the pain and burden, and feeling satisfied with the efforts I was making on her behalf.

Jonathan arrived on 14 August. He weighed only 6 lbs, a tiny scrap of humanity, and was nursed in the special care baby unit as he was jaundiced. I was not allowed any real contact with him except to be pushed into the unit by wheelchair and watch him through a glass porthole. Evidently jaundiced babies are extra-sensitive to picking up infections and have to be looked after in this special way. I heard dismal stories from the nurses that he would not take a bottle and was losing weight, and so on the fourth day I presented myself at the door of the unit and informed the sister in charge that this was my baby and if they could not manage to feed him then I insisted on breast-feeding him myself, and yes, I did appreciate that I would have to wear a gown and a mask but I was going to feed him.

Sister was rather taken aback by this intrusion into the privacy of her special ward, but she agreed, and from that day Jonathan and I became united and my fighting spirit returned. I was over-protective towards him, rather like a lioness protecting her cubs. I was not at all happy for anybody else to handle him. He was all mine, terribly special, and while I had him with me, while I cuddled and nursed him, I felt a strong contact with John. Surely this little boy was an extension of him.

The ten days in hospital were an escape from the stresses and strains of the last year, the first break I had had since John's illness. Other mothers were anxious to return home as quickly as possible. I made the most of the opportunity for somebody else to look after the baby, somebody else to bring me meals, and take away the responsibilities even if only for a short time.

The hospital arranged a car service to take us home, where my mother was waiting to provide the comfort and love which she always gave to us all so unconditionally. I often wonder what I would have done without her.

Those early months with Jonathan as a tiny baby were not particularly difficult. Clare and Mark were delighted with the new baby, Clare in a protective, fussing, feminine way, Mark just pleased that it was a brother. It was a blessing that I had Jonathan to keep me busy and occupied by day, so that there was little time to brood over my thoughts when the other children were at school. The doctor had provided a home help for me three mornings a week, so most of the heavy household chores were done, which helped immensely.

I took part in village activities, joined a few women's clubs and decided that I would not return to London after all. Country life had grown on me. I would make a life for us all here, Essex was where we all belonged, the memories that London held for me were of my life with John, and that could never be.

John's mother, Nana Bispham, as she was called (Bispham being the family name), visited us often. She never got over the death of her son and had frequent periods of severe depression, even attempting to take her own life on several occasions. She had so loved her son, had suffered with him all through his painful childhood, and then just as he had something wonderful to live for, as she said, it all had to be taken away. She never said a bad word about me, everything I did was always perfect, my cooking was wonderful, and as for the way I brought the children up, well, nobody could have done it better. I really did love her and she tried so hard, even though she was at times so confused and ill, to give me every possible help and encouragement.

She could not pick Jonathan up without floods of tears, particularly when he reached six months and his eyes became the darkest brown and had a real twinkle in them when he smiled. 'He is John's double,' she would say. 'John's eyes were large and brown like that when he was this age.'

I shall always remember Nana Bispham as a wonderfully warm person. It was sad that after John's death she spent most of her life in and out of psychiatric hospitals. Although I frequently took the children to visit her, she became increasingly confused and eventually had to be admitted on a permanent basis. She lived to be 90, but for the last ten years of her life she did not recognise anyone and reverted to a childlike state. It was probably the kindest thing that could have happened, as it freed her from the grief and anguish that tormented her day after day in her heartbroken condition.

The physical problems involved in rearing Jonathan were exactly the same as before, only I had become adept in coping with difficult situations, the main one being lifting him from the floor. So back we went to the cloth harness. I could then grab him, even from a sitting position, and hoist him up on to my lap. Changing his nappy and dressing him was made simple by converting an old tea trolley. I lined the top level with thick foam, and then laid him upon this, while the bottom tier held nappies, powder and a change of clothes.

Jonathan did not adapt very well to changing from breast milk to cow's milk and I am sure this was the start of his allergic reaction to cow's milk, which was manifested in him as eczema. Very soon his legs and ankles were very red and itchy and were treated by the doctor with cortisone creams, which I now realise was given out far too liberally.

That first year flew by, it was a progressive year, a year of rebuilding my life from the shattering events of the previous one. I was kept very busy, for I am a great believer that hard work cures many problems. Yet I wanted more purpose in life. I found living in a small cul-de-sac in a tiny village restricting, and I also wanted to find ways of adding to my income which only covered general expenses. Nothing was left over for any extras and certainly nothing could be put by as a reserve.

Through a friend I heard of a much larger property for sale just three miles away, still in a village, but nearer to towns and facilities. The house had a large ground-floor extension. I went to see it and decided that it would be perfect as I could let the top and live in the bottom. It had a nice garden and was surrounded by fields, so that wherever you looked you saw fields with grazing for horses in the back and cornfields in the front. It also had the benefit of a large drive. I always remember that for all that accommodation the asking price was £7,500 and I offered £7,250. My father kindly lent me the extra amount needed, and I decided to buy it and take in paying guests which would provide me with an income and also give me some company. I called the house Heathfield.

10 Heathfield

We moved into Heathfield in 1968. It turned out to be a good move, providing me with both some adult company and an income which proved to be far more remunerative than I ever imagined.

The previous owner, a Mrs White, had had a young American boy living with the family for a couple of years, and she asked me if I would be prepared to keep him on. He had a bedroom on the top floor. Mike was an extremely nice young man, he was only 20 and just had his evening meal with us. I put an advertisement in the local paper which brought several enquiries from students or business people needing accommodation for short or long periods, so then I let the second bedroom. These paying guests were the answer to several of my problems. They were nice people who were quite happy for me to go out in the evenings, so I had on-the-spot free baby-sitters. The extra money eased my finances, provided extra treats for the family and enabled me to build up a little nest egg.

I found a very capable woman to help me with housework, so all I had to do was to prepare large quantities of good home-cooked food, which I was now quite good at.

I fell in love with Heathfield, if one can ever really fall in love with a house. The views were breath-taking. From the three bedrooms upstairs all that could be seen was undisturbed views of miles of country, fields of horses and in the far distance the odd farmhouse.

The ground floor extension meant that we had four large rooms, kitchen, bathroom and separate cloakroom. The kitchen faced a field and you could actually touch the horses from the kitchen window. To be able to wake up each morning to horses nuzzling the fence, to watch the harvesting in the autumn and the planting of the fields in the spring was such a welcome sight and a far cry from London, which I knew I would never return to. Life in the country suited my personality far more than London ever did. To be surrounded by so much space somehow made me feel more in tune with nature.

The garden was large, so I had to have help with that. We had a septic tank for our sewage and drainage, which turned out to be quite temperamental. Everything worked well until we had a heavy rainfall, then all of a sudden you would see a thin stream of soapsuds from the washing machine drift over the garden, which meant that the septic tank was having a job coping with the quantities of excess water, and we frequently had to have the system drained. The beauty of the septic tank was that we grew the most magnificent vegetables. Whether they liked the frequent baths of soap that they had or whether the well-manured soil had anything to do with it I shall never know, but we had everything from runner beans to cauliflowers. Even the fruit trees produced magnificent crops. It was a real 'Garden of Eden'.

Jonathan walked during his second summer at Heathfield. He was a lovely-looking child, dark-haired, dark-skinned with brown twinkling eyes. His health was far from robust and he had frequent eruptions of irritating eczema which broke out mainly on his legs, hands and feet. Skin creams relieved him only for a short period. From a very early age he used to play for hours with his toys, building blocks, miniature cars; he was a very easy little boy who amused himself.

I had made one special friend during my new life in Essex. I met Margaret at the ante-natal clinic and our babies were born just a few days apart – she had a son as well. We formed a very close friendship, and she was a great help and support to me during those years on my own. Once a week we had lunch together, she was very good at hairdressing and used to set my hair, and our boys grew up and went to playgroup together and we had a lot of fun. She was always willing to look after my family, and I helped out as much as possible in looking after hers. Within the next few years she gave birth to two lovely daughters. Their life always seemed to me then to be ideal. They lived in a lovely large house with an enormous garden. Her husband was a commercial artist and so their decor was exquisite: beautiful colour schemes, curtains and carpets that matched perfectly. Even their garden was a picture and hardly had a weed.

It was Margaret who encouraged me to join Weight Watchers, and I shall be eternally grateful to her for this. I had been overweight for years. Despite not being a fish and chip or junk food eater and certainly not being brought up to a suet pudding diet, I had always found it hard to shed those pounds. Now that I had baby-sitters available most evenings I could quite easily go out once or twice a week, and so I joined Weight Watchers and became very involved with this disciplined, caring organisation. They really understood fat people, and the weekly classes, the excellent diet, and working together with a group of people who all had the same problem cetainly worked. Within six months of joining I had shed 40lbs and looked so much younger, and felt fitter than I had for years. The loss of weight obviously gave me increased mobility.

The Weight Watchers Organisation were trying to get suitable

My grandmother

My parents celebrating their Golden Wedding, July 1987

Bonnie made an excellent 'foot muff' while I was writing my book

Husband John aged eleven

John after we were married

My brother Tony

Richard with his son Richard

Four-year-old Clare and six-year-old Mark

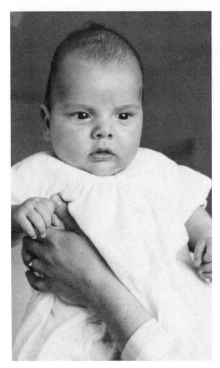

Jonathan at six weeks

In the garden at Heathfield with three-month-old Heather

Twenty-eight-year-old Mark

Twenty-one-year-old Jonathan

Seventeen-year-old Heather

Clare and her husband John

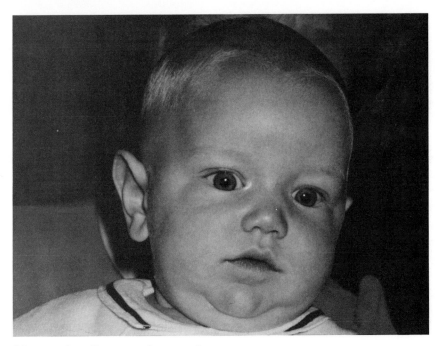

My grandson James at five months

My great friend Maurice and, above, the beautiful farmhouse where he and his family lived

members to train as group area lecturers and particularly were interested in anyone who had teaching or lecturing experience. I decided that this was right up my street and applied for training, which involved going to London one day a week for ten weeks. I found the training fascinating; we studied diet, psychology, and the basic management of a class. Six months later I was given the opportunity to start my first class in Bishop's Stortford, Herts. This little class of fat ladies grew rapidly to a large class of rapidly reducing ladies, so I was working in a semi-medical caring capacity where diplomacy, tact and an understanding nature were constantly called for. One quickly learns that fat people certainly are never 'happy' about their size, and that grossly overweight people always have some strong psychological problem which causes them to resort to food for comfort. Frustration, lack of love, a poor opinion of themselves – there is always something. I eventually had two classes under my care. Monthly staff meetings were held in London. These were semi-business-cum-social affairs which I looked forward to. I ran these classes for years.

Heathfield was beautiful in spring, summer and autumn and I even loved it in the winter when the wind howled around, and when some mornings there was a thick fog that restricted any view for hours. There were times after a thick fall of snow when we were cut off for sometimes two days at a time, but I still loved it.

I had probably covered a lot of ground in those last two years, had got over the initial pain of bereavement, remembering the happy and eventful times in our marriage more frequently than the suffering and loneliness associated with John's death. Though Jonathan's birth had been another traumatic and emotional experience, in a unique way he compensated for the loss of John as well as keeping me very busy and occupied.

The children joined in with village activities, and made new friends. The little village school was a friendly happy environment, where, because of the limited numbers, every child could be an individual, and they did teach the basic three Rs which I am totally in favour of. Clare joined the Brownies, Mark the Cubs. We went to church on Sundays, to that beautiful peaceful old church surrounded by enormous old trees, right in the middle of a heath. On Sundays the local cricket club played, and strawberry and cream teas were available at some of the big houses in the summer. It really was a typical English village.

In some ways I suppose that when you live in a village you are escaping into another world. We lived lives which were more peaceful and on the right lines. It was a complete change from the suburban atmosphere in which we had lived in London, with a husband in a profession, and busy shops, street lights, heavy traffic hurtling past every day casting its heavy fumes over everybody and everything.

Although there were times when I feared that children being brought up solely by a mother suffered, I used to console myself with the fact that thousands of children were fatherless in the war and they had turned out all right. I really think that the person who suffers most in this situation is the mother, as she has so many roles to fulfil – mother, father, provider, nurse, counsellor. So much is demanded and taken for granted, yet children cannot be expected to understand the heavy burden of responsibility and the strain that their mother is constantly under. You are giving of yourself all the time, but the comforts and pleasures of marriage are no longer yours. There is no one to share the responsibility and the decisions, and no respite from the work or the worry.

If anyone asked me for my opinion on single-parent families, I would say it is the most difficult situation for any woman to be in, trying to make a good job of bringing up her family on her own.

11 Second time around

As a widow I was not locked into the enclosed world of feeling that no other man could ever make me happy, that I would never marry again. The thought of a solitary life at the age of 30 was to me a 'fate worse than death'.

Richard came into my life when he telephoned about the accommodation I had to offer. He was a man of 35 with a Scots accent, a very grim expression and a rather withdrawn personality, and a nervous abrupt manner. He took the accommodation very happily and a friendship quickly developed between us. Once we got to know each other he lost his tension and was friendly and caring. Looking back I suppose we were both in a vulnerable emotional situation; it was only two years since John's death and Richard had very recently separated from his wife after what seemed to be a rather disastrous short marriage, the only positive aspect of which seemed to be the birth of their son Richard. Richard said that he fell in love with me the moment we met and knew that above all else he wanted me for the rest of his life.

He did so much for me, including decorating the whole house inside and out. I have never seen anybody put such love and care into decorating – his work was perfection – and I knew that if I had asked for a ceiling to be painted with royal blue stars, he would have been only too pleased to do that as well.

It was a bonus for me to have, for the first time in my life, a physical tower of strength to lean on. Richard was a stockily built, physically strong man who had spent many years in Scotland in the Forestry Commission, planting trees and working outside most of the time.

Richard's childhood seemed to have been a very hard experience both physically and mentally. His father left the family and went off to South Africa when he was three and his sister only two. His mother had to struggle as a cook/housekeeper to many large estates in Scotland. Because she was so good at her job and was hard to replace she was allowed to keep the children with her but she had to maintain good relationships with the gentry and make sure that the children were seen and not heard. I suppose the alternative would have been to place them in care. I know that Richard's childhood was plagued with fears of homelessness and insecurity, and he grew up in a clinical atmosphere of 'pomp and ceremony' with lots of stringent rules and regulations and always the fear that his mother would lose her job and they would be homeless. His childhood had been as insecure as mine had been, though for a different reason.

Apart from the strain on the children it must have been a terrible situation for his mother. I am sure that she really loved her children but somehow I always felt that they had been starved of much affection or closeness and both Richard and his sister seemed to have difficulty in expressing their feelings, and they also found the expression of affection by others embarrassing.

I found his mother a very withdrawn tight-lipped person, embittered by her hard life (and probably justifiably so). She had such sad eyes; she had been deeply in love with her first husband whom she never saw again. When Richard was 11, his mother married again. Unfortunately, it turned out that her new husband was an unbalanced character and there were a lot of bizarre behavioural problems which no doubt had a disastrous effect on two young children. I feel that we are all 'victims of our childhood'. That marriage ended in divorce in a very short time.

Both Richard and his sister were super-efficient people. Sylvia ran her home well and had three children, Neil the eldest and then two daughters Fiona and Ruth. I liked the children but always felt the lack of any 'gentleness or love' – again there seemed to be lots of rules and strict discipline.

Richard's son, always known as 'little Richard', was seven when we first met. He had a thick head of auburn curls, lots of freckles and we all liked him. Mentally he was rather slow, the reason for which was thought to be the fact that he was born prematurely and had had problems with breathing. This little chap had to go to a 'special needs school'. He had poor communication and co-ordination but young Richard and I eventually had a very close relationship and I felt that my children and myself contributed much to encourage his self-confidence, which was sorely lacking. He responded so quickly to any expression of affection that I could not help wondering if he had ever had any real love from either of his parents. He had been well cared for, fed and watered but then you can offer that service to a pot plant.

At the time that we met, Richard was in an industrial position as a transport manager and was studying for his transport examinations. He really was such a grafter, working in a full-time job, going to evening school to study with the Institute of Transport and working to do things in the home and garden at weekends. From his humble beginnings in the Forestry Commission, where he spent most of his time planting Christmas trees and working on the land, he had done exceedingly well.

Richard loved and needed me with an almost desperate urgency. As he said, 'You are as essential to me as the very air I breathe.' He accepted my children, which was probably difficult for him, especially as it meant sharing my affection with three very different characters who all needed it too. For me he meant freedom from physical struggle, somebody to lift and carry, take responsibilities and, most important of all, he loved me and I loved him in return, although, if I am honest with myself, I was sometimes nervous of him when he retreated into his shell of silence when problems arose – and I was aware of having to be careful what I said to avoid his over-reaction to situations. Nevertheless we did have many happy times, holidays and outings with the children, things that I would not have been able to provide for them. We did get married, only a very small quiet affair with just a few friends as we had already been living together for two years waiting for Richard's divorce.

He desperately wanted a child of his own, firstly I suppose to assure himself that he could have a bright intelligent child and secondly as an obvious expression of our love. Heather was born in March 1972. Richard chose her name because he said Heather reminded him so much of Scotland. This pregnancy was different. There was somebody around to care for and support me, someone in whom to confide all my fears and trepidations. The pregnancy proved difficult – my back ached constantly and my mobility was very much reduced during the last three months. Really, I had overdone it, I had put too much strain on an already damaged body, but we wanted this child and it was vital that he have a child of his own, particularly as he was involved with my three.

Unfortunately he was not very supportive about labour, and he was certainly not around until well after she was born so the birth was another lonely experience. However, I accepted his explanation that he could not bear to watch somebody he loved in pain.

I felt ill after having Heather. I had lost a lot of blood and was so weak that I could not hold a cup of tea. I was totally uninterested in this baby, in some way almost blaming her for my sorry state. Richard was overjoyed at having a daughter and this time I did get the red roses and the lovely cards, so somehow I came to terms with his lack of emotional support and silently forgave him.

We had some happy years at Heathfield, leading a simple life. Richard was striving for his final examinations and I was occupied with a home to run and four children during the week plus Richard's son at the weekends. We did not have much but we were contented.

There were times in our marriage when I longed to break down the high wall that Richard had erected around himself. I found communication on a personal level impossible. He retreated into his 'silent world' when any problems arose in the family and he and Clare had constant battles. I always seemed to be doing a 'juggling act', trying to keep the peace and find a balance. I feel sure that his own mother reacted in a similar way when emotional problems arose when he and his sister were children, cold silence, a withdrawal of love – I could not bear it.

I always felt that Richard was two people; he could be loving, understanding and oversensitive, or totally pig-headed and cold, imposing ridiculous standards on how we should all live. This meant there were always big divisions between us on discipline. I loved the soft, loving man that he could be, but I hated the arrogant intolerant man that he often was. I felt that he considered 'softness of character' as being 'weak' and aggression and strictness as being 'hard'. I believe that in fact the opposite is true. Over the years I have met many people who were brought up in rather a cold, strict atmosphere and I have always found them to be lacking in self-confidence, with poor communication skills.

The five children got on well. There was no trouble at all there, but frequently I fought an inner battle about whom I owed most loyalty to, who came first, and I have to admit that I always protected my own flesh and blood. They came first, I could not help it; like an animal with its young, I was fiercely defensive of them and proud of it.

12 Changes

As soon as Heather became active and started walking and the older children started senior school, we decided to move from Heathfield and bought a more modern house just a few miles away but nearer to Harlow. I never realised just how much I would miss Heathfield, the breathtaking views, being surrounded by so much space, even the horses in the adjoining field. However, there were many practical problems to be sorted out. Transport from the village was extremely limited, so that in order for the older children to join in any after-school activities or clubs either Richard or I had to act as a transport service. There were no street lights in the village and even going to the village centre in the winter time meant an absolutely pitch-black walk on a rough grass track and I worried about the dangers involved.

The house we bought was not particularly large, but it was comfortably placed in a small cul-de-sac, and it did back on to a field once again. The most important feature was that buses ran from the end of the road, setting the children free to get out and about by themselves without danger.

We made several improvements to the house, including a new kitchen, and we added an extra room on the ground floor to give us more space. Heather was just under a year old when we made our move, and so the extension proved to be a useful room where toys could be kept, and all the messy games that children revelled in could take place. Lego and Playdoh, I think, were always the favourites. Being a modern house it was much easier to keep clean and the garden was quite small in comparison with the half-acre we had had at Heathfield. For weeks and weeks I pined for Heathfield, wished we had never moved but gradually the conveniences proved so beneficial and the work-load so much easier that I managed to get the whole position into better perspective.

Money was short at that time. We had a large family between us, plus Richard's ex-wife and son, and so I decided to find some sort of secretarial work. Within a few weeks I noticed that our local hospital, only 10 minutes away, was advertising for part-time secretaries. I had some limited medical knowledge from my work with Weight Watchers and although they really wanted somebody experienced in the medical field they did offer me the job and agreed to take me on for training.

My job was to work for the neurologist, an absolutely charming lady who needed a secretary for her department just four days a week, 9 to 4. This suited me admirably and I found the work fascinating. Somehow I always felt 'at home' in the medical environment. Within a short time I became familiar with the medical jargon, borrowed a lot of medical books on anatomy and physiology plus neurology from the medical library and studied hard.

Heather was looked after by a good friend of mine who was a registered child-minder. As there was another child of similar age for her to play with, she seemed quite content about the arrangement and 'Aunty Pat' became very special in her life. The extra money relieved some of the financial pressure and made it possible to have a little spare money from time to time without always struggling to make ends meet. If I cut my lunch hour by 15 minutes and left at 3.45, I could just get home as the children got off the school bus.

Our marriage still had far too many tensions in it for my liking. I appreciated that all relationships suffer various stresses and second marriages with combined families create even more, but I never did find a way to cope with the family problems that arose mainly with Clare and Richard.

We had a lot of interests in common, again a love of good music, theatre, country life and, although Richard was rather a loner and I am a born extrovert, when we were on our own we got on well, but within the family situation I was always fighting a battle between his viewpoint about things and mine which were nearly always the opposite.

However, his loyalty to me, his constant attention to my physical needs were always to the fore and I always said, and still do, that if either of my two sons grew up to do just one quarter of the things that he did for me, when I'm old, I would be a very lucky woman. I was very moved when he said, 'If ever you have to go into a wheelchair when you are older, I will be first in the queue to push it.' Words no other man has ever said to me.

Looking back on all this now, I feel that my way was the 'right way' for I have four children who have not only all grown up to be highly successful in their chosen careers, but are warm, loving people who are surrounded by friends and enjoy a good quality of life.

The greatest compliment I ever received was when my last child, Heather, left senior school. The headmaster called me into his office and said, 'It has been a privilege to have your children here; they are all very special people who will all go a long way.' The same was said when the boys left the grammar school.

Though I knew in my heart that I would not end my days with Richard, it was as a desperate last attempt to improve our lifestyle, to enable him to leave his job in industry which he disliked immensely, that we decided to buy a village shop and Post Office. Looking back it was the most crazy thing we ever did. It did have a large five-bedroomed house attached to it, so we moved to this new dream to another mass of decorating and improvements. The plan was for Richard to run the shop and Post Office with the staff that were already there. However, my intuition told me to keep Richard in his job for at least three months to see how things went. Regardless of what the accounts revealed, there was no way that this shop was going to give us the income we had at the moment, so I left my hospital job and tried to run the shop, which physically and mentally nearly killed me. So all that the new venture created was another load of strain and tension to an already strained relationship.

I did not blame Richard, in fact I took more of the blame myself, for I should never have agreed to the shop in the first place. Consequently we were both hellishly bad-tempered, me through exhaustion, he through the worry of how we were going to get rid of it.

The summer of 1975 happened to be very hot and everything that could go wrong did. The deep freeze broke down and so did the large fridge. We had a major problem with a blocked sewer, Heather fell downstairs and broke her arm, Jonathan fell against a plate glass door and severely cut his ankle, missing the artery by a fraction, so he had to go to hospital to have several stitches in the very deep wound. Shortly after that episode he was taken ill with a severe attack of asthma which took him rapidly into hospital.

Our evenings were spent going to the Cash & Carry to replenish the stocks and our weekends trying to balance the books for the Post Office, which was not an easy task. How I would have loved to have crept back into the security of the womb during this period of my life, to have been completely divorced from all that was going on around me.

The shop would have to go, that was a certainty, even if we did lose a lot of money and despite the fact that we had been there for only six months. We put the shop up for sale with a local agent. By an extremely lucky set of circumstances a viewer came round, a local man, who wanted a shop as a stop-gap between ending his own large business and starting his retirement. He had a bungalow to sell and by an even stranger coincidence the bungalow was almost opposite the house we had sold just a few months before. The bungalow had a lovely setting, standing in a third of an acre, but it was rather on the small side. It had only three bedrooms, one of which was very small, so it would mean building on again! We decided on a mutual exchange which was the easiest way out of the situation and would save us both stamp duty.

We moved in January 1976 after a traumatic experience which was entirely of our own making. We really did get all we deserved in buying that stupid shop. I think Richard settled back into his job with an entirely different attitude. It had taught him a lesson and made him thankful for what he had, a good job in industry, company car and all the fringe benefits of a commercial concern.

I re-applied to the hospital for another vacancy and this time worked for a psychiatrist, which was not quite so interesting as my last job, but at least I was lucky enough to be accepted back into the hospital away from that dreadful shop and I was involved with suffering humanity which was an area where I knew I belonged.

I have not referred to my brother Tony since the beginning of this book, not because he had disappeared from the face of the earth, but because he and I had little in common at that time in our lives. He was totally unconventional, not really interested in family life and children, and visited us only occasionally. He had devoted his working career to training as a wig-maker and he was good at his trade.

He also had a compassionate interest in spirituality, alternative medicine which I knew nothing about, and it was at this time that he introduced me to Reflexology. This is a therapy which works on the principle that there are minute reflex points in the feet which have a relativity to each and every organ, function and part of the body. By applying a refined pressure to these reflex points a stimulation occurs which frees the body from congestion, has a great relaxing ability and enables the body to 'heal itself'. Reflexology has similarities to acupuncture apart from the fact that no needles are used, and the feet are the only areas to be worked upon – in fact it was often referred to in ancient times as 'acupuncture without the use of needles'. I was originally sceptical about how working on somebody's feet could have an effect on the body, but nevertheless I was willing to listen and learn, particularly when Tony mentioned how beneficial it was in treating asthma. It seemed at the time as if we were clutching at straws, but Jonathan's health was so poor and so little improvement seemed to have been achieved by the specialists at the Chest Hospital that I would have tried anything.

Reflexology had evidently been founded in Egypt some 2,500 years ago but in more recent times, 1937, in fact, it had been revived by an American physical therapist called Eunice Ingham and it was quite widely known in both America and Canada, but was completely unknown in Britain. I read, enthralled, Eunice Ingham's book on the subject, *Stories the Feet Can Tell*. Tony brought me a large coloured foot chart showing exactly how the body is mirrored in the feet and how the feet reflect the disfunctions within by revealing a sensitivity in their extremities, and how if we apply an alternating pressure on these sensitive areas, it stimulates almost an 'electric charge' through the nerve centres in the body. I found it all quite fascinating and was eager for Tony to work on Jonathan's feet.

Within three months of Jonathan's starting to have regular treatment, there was a tremendous change in the severity of his asthma attacks. For the first time in many years, he was off all drugs. There was a certain 'bloom' that appeared on him and he was far more energetic and fit than he had ever been before. I was still sceptical, wondering if it were coincidence but I was quite moved when he said that after he had a treatment he felt 'well all over'. His twice-weekly Reflexology session was not a chore as perhaps one might have thought it would be for a young boy of just eight, it was an event which he looked forward to.

Everybody knows everybody in a small village, and ours was no exception. Mothers I met at the school and friends and acquaintances that I had met over the years all remarked on the improvement in Jonathan's health. 'Was it some new wonder drug?' they asked. 'What's happened? He is like a new child.'

I was embarrassed, embarrassed to say 'Well, it's this Reflexology', because I did not know enough about it to involve myself in a discussion. Fifteen years ago it was a totally unknown subject, and sadly it is still not very well known even today, although interest in all forms of alternative medicine is growing rapidly.

When I explained in my limited way that in order to help the body heal itself you work upon the feet with a specialised pressure therapy, there was a lot of bewilderment. However, some did listen. Outside the village school therefore became the meeting-place for informal talks about Reflexology.

Apart from his new-found improved health, Jonathan's school work improved remarkably now that he was off all suppressant drugs, inhalers, steroids and getting a good night's sleep. He was able to show his real potential, the abilities that I, as his mother, knew that he had. That fine creative brain burst into action, rather like releasing the brakes on a car, and within that year he went right to the top of the class.

I shall always be eternally grateful to my brother for pointing me in the right direction towards a fulfilling career, a new way of life, in the field of healing. I had always been interested in people and medicine but was beginning to realise that the hospital environment was not the right direction for me. I feel also that Reflexology brought far more happiness and fulfilment into my life than it ever did for my brother, although he was to become a first-class therapist and an excellent tutor. He was the instigator who lit the flame within me that was to fire me with the power and enthusiasm I was to need for the rest of my life.

It was a sad time for the whole family when Mum's brother, George, died in an Asian flu epidemic. A sudden very severe attack of the illness caused severe inflammation of his lungs and nothing could be done to save him. He was only 57 at the time and left a wife and two young daughters, Tracey and Elizabeth. My mother, who had always been very close to her brother, found the suddenness of his death a great shock and hard to bear.

Gran died not long afterwards in March 1975. She was staying temporarily in a nursing home while my mother was on holiday and although she had managed for years on her own in an old cottage with a flight of steep stairs, ironically she fell backwards down a few stairs in the nursing home and fractured her pelvis. Pneumonia set in and she died very quickly. She was 92, yet when the post-mortem was performed because of her unexpected death, there was no evidence of any disease in her body, her heart, lungs, kidneys, were all sound and certainly not as usually found in a person of that age. All the disability she suffered was mild arthritis in her hands; she had become very deaf, and her eyesight was failing.

My mother and her sister arranged to sell Gran's house in Kent and all her belongings. I was very pleased that my mother was able to keep the chiming clock with its large brass numerals, as this old clock would always be a great reminder of Gran.

My mother gave my brother and me a share in the sum that was realised and with this unexpected windfall Richard and I decided to buy a caravan as a way of having reasonably cheap holidays with such a large family. We bought our caravan with its awning to sleep the older children and all the equipment necessary for a caravanning holiday.

We decided on Scotland. Inverness was our ultimate destination, Richard having spent a lot of his childhood there. He had moved to Scotland with his mother and sister when he was just 11 and from those formative early years no doubt Scotland was in his blood. I was just as enthusiastic about visiting Scotland as he as I loved mountains and lochs.

We really were rather too ambitious in the distance involved in getting there with a caravan as Heather was only 18 months old and it meant that she had to sit restrained in her pram in the back of our estate car for long periods of time.

Our first stopping-place was the Yorkshire Dales. We stayed in a superb caravan park, spotlessly clean, with very few inhabitants and a delightful Pets' Corner that kept the children interested and happy for hours.

We should have stayed in Yorkshire, as that would have been quite far enough, but the aim was Scotland, so that was where we went. Richard had an old friend who had a sheep farm in Fort William. He also owned a caravan park alongside the farm and we had reserved a space there weeks before. The traffic was murderous, the heat intense, and we ended up with a car load of cranky children and a yelling baby. We endured a three-hour traffic jam getting from Inverness to Fort William.

After a lot of trouble we eventually found the caravan park. Richard's friend was nowhere to be found and nobody knew anything about a reservation for us. The caravan park was packed, there was not an inch of space. By this time it was early evening and we knew that if we could not find somewhere to park for the night soon we were going to be in trouble. We seemed to drive for miles before we noticed a sign saying 'Caravan space to let' and pulled in to a run-down old farmhouse. Eventually a farmer came out of the house complete with kilt, sporran and all, and spoke to us in very broad Scots, so broad that we could hardly understand a word that he said.

Richard seemed to understand him well, and he directed us around a bend in which he said we would find a small field where we could park. We found the field, it was small and empty, but to my horror it was on the top of a mountain with a drop of several hundred feet.

'It's no good, we are not staying there even if only for one day, it would be a nightmare keeping an eye on Heather all the time. We will just have to move on,' I said, 'and find something else.'

We were all despondent, hot, tired, thirsty, and I would have given anything for a bath and a cup of English tea.

We drove on for miles. I felt sorry for Richard, who had been behind that wheel pulling a caravan all day, and was desperately in need of a rest. After at least another ten miles we pulled up at another croft with a notice outside, 'Caravan Park'. By this time it was dusk, but luckily there was a small space in this already packed caravan site. It was dirty and had few conveniences, but it was better than nothing. However, it was about 9 o'clock when the farmer came out of his croft into the caravan park and set light to huge piles of rubbish which were piled up in large drums. For the rest of that night and even into the next morning everything was covered with debris from the fire, there were smuts on everything, on our faces, clothes, all over the caravan, the car, everything was covered in black smuts. Heather looked as if she had been up a chimney. We all went to the archaic shower, which was a hut with wooden boards and a shower which reluctantly pumped out brownish water, but it was better than nothing.

The following morning Richard took the two boys off fishing just to break the apathy that prevailed. Life seemed much brighter when they brought back two trout. Moving on, we eventually found a reasonably safe, clean site where we stayed for the rest of our holiday, which was pleasant and reasonably peaceful.

When we returned home we let our caravan out to various people for a few months and then, deciding that caravanning did not give quite the freedom that we had anticipated, we sold it. In future, we decided, holidays with less driving for Richard and fewer domestic chores for me would be the order of the day.

However, it was an experience, and I really did love Scotland!

13 Joyce

Joyce came into my life when I employed her to help me in the house. It may seem strange to devote a chapter to an individual who cleaned your house but Joyce was unique. Eccentric as she was and still is, she still retains a place in my heart. Never before have I met anyone whose needs of life were so small and whose happiness could be so easily achieved.

Joyce had been born in Old Harlow, and had married David, a kind man with a quiet loving, disposition. He had come from a family of gentlemen farmers, was still very attractive in his sixties, so must have been quite a catch in his earlier years. Joyce was so different from him. She could be extremely firey on occasions and she certainly called 'a spade a spade'.

Joyce and David had always lived with her parents, and had managed to enjoy a happy life with the four of them living under the same roof. They had two children, first a son, David, and then a daughter, Jane. Grandma had brought the children up as Joyce had not much interest in bringing up children. Although she was kindness itself, being restricted in the home for hours on end looking after a baby would not have been her ideal occupation, so Grandma looked after the children during the day and Joyce went to work in a factory.

Joyce had a passion for animals that I have never come across before. She was a real St Francis and had a way with all animals which came first in her life, with people a definite second. She loved the fields, the woods and space and she was very much in tune with nature.

Joyce was very tall and angular, as strong as an ox. Her face had a fine bone structure and she wore her thick grey hair piled up on top in a knot. I am sure she was very handsome in her younger days. She worried constantly about her health and always imagined and exaggerated some slight ache or pain as 'being the worst', whatever the worst was, and dreaded illness and death.

She wore strange concoctions of clothes and was very proud of her attendance at all the 'aristocratic' jumble sales as she called them. She would scan through the local newspaper on a Friday evening to see where jumble sales were being held, and if they were in a very 'upper class' village, off she would go with David and come back with lots of good, hardly worn clothes. Sometimes she wore a tweed skirt with bright blue lacy tights and brogues, and during the summer she would walk out with a parasol and a large straw sun-hat, always with a dog on a lead and sometimes somebody's else's too.

All animals, she insisted, were not looked after properly by their owners. The only animals that were properly cared for were hers. Her dogs were walked more than any other dogs that I have ever known. They were fed on chicken or best liver, while Joyce and David had sausages. Joyce's dogs had sheepskin-lined coats, fur-lined baskets for the winter and were loved and adored every minute of every day.

While she was helping me in the mornings she was quite convinced that I had forgotten to feed the cat, or our dog, Nicki, and although I assured her that they had been fed just an hour ago, as soon as I was out of the room, she would take another tin of food out of the cupboard and re-feed both of them saying that 'The poor things look starving!'

She would go up to complete strangers and ask them if they were aware that their dog barked frequently during the day and threaten to report them to the RSPCA, as it was just cruelty to leave a dog inside all day while you worked.

She would free dogs from leashes if she found them restrained in their gardens while their owners were out. One day I saw her with four dogs on leads and when I asked her where they came from, she confided that they were barking and terribly sad in their gardens. Their owners were at work, so she just had to go in and take them out for a walk, but she was certainly going to return them to the right house in an hour or so.

If she caught children dragging a dog along on a lead or ill-treating an animal in any way, she placed her curse upon them and had no hesitation at all in giving them 'a piece of her mind'. I shall never forget the time when a group of youngsters fired pellets at the pigeons which were perched on the church tower. She hurled such abuse at them that she absolutely terrorised those youngsters, which had far more effect than the local policeman. They certainly never repeated their antics.

She really became known as the 'village eccentric'. On cold winters' nights she would go out and place saucers of warm milk under the lamp-posts in case there were any starving cats about.

Whether it be a rabbit, a mouse or a horse, Joyce would be there checking up on its general state of health and caring.

In later years she became the proud possessor of a goat, and it was quite normal to see her taking the goat for a walk on a lead and carrying, or rather dragging, great branches from trees for it to eat. The goat absolutely ruined their garden, which just became a sea of mud. A wooden shed was erected for the goat to protect her from bad weather, but later Joyce condescended to allow the goat to take up a new residence at the back of the old village pub where there was a large field, given over as a smallholding. This was owned by the publican and was of great interest to all the local people as it had a vast selection of animals, from cattle to peacocks, so the goat had her new location. However, Joyce was not at all happy about the goat's welfare and every morning she would be up by 6 and over in the field tending and feeding the goat. She also took on the responsibility of looking after the other goats, chickens and ducks. They were groomed daily and she supplied sacks of goat mix, plus corn for the chickens, all from her own very limited pocket.

Joyce needed nothing at all materially, only the oldest pair of shoes she could find and the freedom to roam the fields in all weathers. She knew all the birds by name, got tremendous pleasure from seeing a baby rabbit or a vole and would tell me of places where she knew foxes had their lairs. Provided she could take with her her beloved dogs, and she had several in her time, then she was happy.

When she worked for me in the house she polished until you could see your face in the dining table, and I had, so she told me, the shiniest taps in the whole village. Nobody could clean taps like Joyce. She really did make my house spotless when she came in twice a week, and took a great pride in what she did.

Dear Joyce, she was with me for fifteen years until she decided in her late sixties that she had had enough of housework and retired. I see her most days, always in the fields, with her dog – this one is a grey whippet.

The only real fear she had was illness or death, saying she could never bear to think about either. She still related the painful death of her mother to whom she was devoted. I do hope that when her time comes she will fade away quietly in her sleep, with her beloved dog by her side. Provided she is surrounded with animals to the very end of her life, she will wish for nothing more.

14 My new world

My brother mentioned to me that training classes in Reflexology were about to start in London. A representative from the American organisation was coming to hold sessions in London. 'Why don't you go and attend a course and see how you get on? You seem so interested and you have proof of its effectiveness in Jon,' said Tony.

The courses cost £40 and we did not have £40. We had just moved into the bungalow and had all the added expenses of a new home, and £40 to spend on a training course seemed a luxury. Then out of the blue a month later I had a £40 tax rebate. Should I buy a new outfit for work which I desperately needed, or should I spend it on a course in Reflexology?

I applied for the course, but even two days before, I almost changed my mind because I felt so guilty about spending that sort of money when we were so very hard up. We always seemed to have an overdraft, no matter how carefully we planned our finances. We just had too many people to support and that was that.

Richard drove me up to London. The course was held in the Londoner Hotel and I was amazed to find that there were nearly 40 people in attendance, all so enthusiastic. Some were young people, some middle-aged and some nearing retirement. Most of the group seemed to have had such a wonderful success with treatment for all manner of illness that the improvement in their health had led them to want to study and help other people. Some of the students had a medical background, in the nursing field or as physiotherapists, and a couple of people were chiropodists.

The tutor at that time was Doreen Bayly, who was really quite old and very frail, but she certainly had a very positive conviction in the wonderful benefits that Reflexology could offer.

I soaked up the information on that course as a sponge soaks up water. The history of Reflexology was fascinating, and the way the feet almost 'mirrored the body' was quite amazing. We worked on each other's feet for practice, and at the end of that weekend I was utterly convinced and quite bowled over at what I had absorbed.

I attended four further courses during that year, at the end of which I knew instinctively that Reflexology was going to be my life, and felt sure that I had been put on this planet to serve mankind in his relief from pain and suffering.

It was 1975 when I obtained my Diploma. I had been practising on the feet of many of my friends and acquaintances and obtained some quite outstanding results.

Richard believed in Reflexology because he found it highly effective in relieving the constipation which had troubled him for most of his life. Jonathan actually had a whole year free from asthma, and although he was never a sports enthusiast he was able to involve himself in some of the school sports, which was a near-miracle as far as we were concerned. During the following year he passed his 11-plus examination and got a place at a grammar school.

It was really quite amusing when we went back to the chest hospital for his annual examination. He always had to blow into a machine to monitor his peak flow of air, and the specialist was absolutely delighted with the improvement. 'Quite remarkable,' he said, 'quite remarkable – those last few drugs we tried certainly have done the trick.'

'He has not had any drugs for 10 months,' I said, 'he is off everything. We have been trying this ancient form of healing, Reflexology. It has very similar connections with acupuncture, you know.' He just did not want to know and held his hands above his head in amazement – he clearly thought that we were all absolutely mad. I did not care what he thought, what he said, or what anybody else felt. My son was well for the first time in his life and that was all that mattered.

It is hard to introduce changes into people's lives without exposing yourself to a lot of criticism and sometimes ridicule, but I did not care about that. I believed in this, just as much as I believed in and loved my music. I had an affinity to this work, and I knew that I was going to devote the rest of my life to healing. But how, oh how, was I going to get a practice going? I was still working at the hospital, where much as I loved the patients, I longed to get my hands on their feet, and of course this could never be. I wanted to be able to leave the hospital and concentrate on Reflexology, yet we could not manage without my salary.

It was quite amusing really how my first real patient came into my life. Our local milk-lady, Mrs Smith, had delivered milk for years and years, but for the last five years or so she had worn a collar for a very painful neck condition, caused originally by a car crash. I wonder, I thought, if she would let me work on her feet? How would she react? After thinking about it for a good couple of weeks, I made up my mind that when she called for her money the next Friday morning I would bring the subject up and watch her reaction.

'How's your neck been lately?' I asked nervously. 'Oh, it's always a problem. I get a lot of pain but somehow you have to learn to live with it.' 'I think it might well be possible to live without it. I am sure I can help,' I said. 'I want to tell you a little about Reflexology.'

She came into our lounge where I showed her the large coloured foot chart which identified all the areas in the body which were manifested in the feet. 'By working on your feet with this fine pressure therapy, we can break down a lot of the tension and congestion in that neck, I am sure, and you will be amazed at how the pain will reduce and, I hope, disappear. Could you come weekly for a month or so? There will be absolutely no charge. I just want to see if I can help.'

'I'll try anything, anything, to get rid of this pain,' she said, and so we set to work.

After the very first treatment she said that she definitely had more movement in her neck and that the pain had reduced considerably. I breathed a sigh of relief.

We went on week after week and at the end of six weeks the result was absolutely amazing. The collar was off, she had 80 per cent movement and no pain at all. Mrs Smith was just over the moon, she could hardly believe it and nor could I. As she went on her rounds delivering and collecting the money at the end of every week, everybody noticed the missing collar, the smile on her face, and how all the tension had gone. Mrs Smith talked about Reflexology at every house she called. At the end of the next month, I had at least ten new patients, all recommended by Mrs Smith. I always say it was 'With compliments from the United Dairies' that my professional practice began!

Ten sick people came to me for treatment and ten well patients left. All had remarkable relief from a wide variety of conditions: bronchitis, back problems, neck conditions, migraine, high blood pressure, to name but a few. The local butcher came with his painful shoulder, the village shop keeper came with his arthritic knees. It was not dolls or animals now that I was healing, it was real people in trouble, people that I could relate to – and maybe because of the ill health that I myself had overcome, I understood their sufferings, their frustrations, their fears.

This was what I wanted. This was where I belonged, in the healing field without a doubt. The workload was getting difficult to cope with, my hospital job was demanding and so was Reflexology but I had to make sure that I could rely on the practice expanding before I could make the decision to leave the hospital. I had to be absolutely sure that Reflexology was going to give me the satisfaction and lifestyle that I could give the whole of myself to.

My Wednesday afternoon free from the hospital which I usually kept for catching up on jobs in the home filled up instead with patients. They all became happy and well and brought me yet more. I then began working two evenings each week, plus my job at the hospital, then added Saturday mornings. Eventually I had quite a long waiting list of desperate people who had tried everything medically and had been 'given up', made redundant, by the National Health Service. Some accepted their sorry plight, some looked for another way out of their suffering and decided to try Reflexology. The most common remark I heard over those next few months was 'If only I had known about this before, I have been suffering for years and just four treatments with you have made me feel a different person'. It is hard to understand how working on people's feet can achieve such miracles.

I met such lovely people during the next year, people who confided in me, trusted me and who considered me their friend. My hands began to develop such fine sensitivity that I felt as if I was almost 'tuning in' to the sick person with a very special sort of intuitive accuracy.

I had been so sure that if I could resolve most of our financial problems, then our marriage must be easier, it must soften the pathway and reduce the stresses, but it really did not seem to make any difference. There was still a big division between our standards and ideas of discipline in bringing up the children. I was far too lenient, he far too hard, and any disagreement always ended in grim silence which seemed to go on for ever; silence, a killer to any relationship.

I started lecturing, giving talks to various societies, particularly Ladies' Clubs. These lectures proved highly successful and led to my being asked to lecture to societies further afield, in London, Cambridge, Colchester. The more I talked about the science that I so loved and believed in, the more Reflexology grew and the more patients I had coming to me.

My brother decided to exhibit at an Alternative Medicine Fair to be held at Alexandra Palace, north London. It was one of the first fairs involving this type of work that had ever been held in Britain, and it turned out an absolute disaster. It had been badly advertised, the television advertising before the event never took place and all in all it was a waste of time.

However, I did meet Stephen and Dorothy Purdew who had just bought a rather run-down health farm, Henlow Grange, in Bedfordshire. They were obviously hoping to attract some clients to the farm, and we got quite closely involved in a discussion about Reflexology, of which they knew little.

It was arranged for me to go to the Grange and give a lecture on

Reflexology and perhaps a few sample treatments to the clients if they were interested. I started going to the Grange the following month. At first it was a once a month attendance, to a very limited audience, but after a short while the demand grew and I used to go weekly. Eventually I had such an enormous attendance that the Grange actually ran out of chairs! I continued going to the Grange for over five years, meeting some fascinating people, many of whom became friends.

I watched the Grange gradually become transformed from a rather dilapidated health farm into the fine establishment that it is today. Unfortunately I had to discontinue going on a regular basis as the pressure of my work grew to such an extent that I ran out of days. However, I do keep in touch with them and now revel in the luxury of going as a client. I always book the room facing the waterfall and it was at the Grange that most of this book has been written. I class my stays there as a retreat. You are pampered, fed on just the right food, there is a super swimming pool, which of course suits me, and every time I leave there I feel as if I have been reborn.

One year from the day that I qualified I gave in my notice at the hospital, much to the amusement and amazement of many. A lot of the staff thought I was stupid – the consultant I worked for, a psychiatrist, even suggested that it might be best if I had a consultation with the psychologist as frequently people who work in the field of psychiatry become disturbed by their jobs and need a little support themselves. Regardless of everything I left the hospital. I was sad to leave my friends, the nurses and doctors whom I had known for five years, but Reflexology was in my blood and I had to devote all of myself to this work.

One dear friend whom I had worked with at the hospital, Jean – she was an excellent secretary and I had treated her for a health problem that had responded well – had faith in what I intended to do. She said, 'Ann, you are going to do so well with this work, I am sure of that, and if the time comes when you need a secretary please give me first refusal.' Jean is my secretary today and has been for many years.

15 Divided lives

By January 1978 my family were growing up rapidly. Mark was 16 and had become interested in the Sciences. He was studying Physics and Chemistry and looking towards a career in that field.

Clare was an outgoing young lady of 14 who led quite a full life with schoolwork and plenty of friends and activities. She enjoyed riding, swimming, and youth clubs.

Jonathan at 10 still maintained his new-found good health and was making tremendous strides in his schooling. Not only was he naturally academic but he had great artistic flair and could draw and paint quite beautifully. It was a joy to see him join in with activities, to be able to go about with his friends on his bike without the constant dreaded attacks of asthma which spoilt everything. It seemed as if he was making up for lost time, a catching-up process both at school and away from it.

Little Heather, now six, had been at full-time school for just over a year. Although she was not too keen at first, she eventually settled down and accepted that school was somewhere she had to go every day, not just when she felt like it. Her young years had been very uneventful, she was a contented, happy little girl who just grew up.

Reflexology was taking over my life. Slowly, slowly, the direction of everything was changing. I can honestly say that it was the only thing that came into my life without me having to go out and fight for it. I found I had a great affinity for feet, an uncanny sensitivity in my hands, a compassion for my fellow man and a restlessness that encouraged me to promote and pioneer this healing work, so that the masses might grow to understand and benefit from this ancient therapy. Reflexology was hardly known in England at that time and was a subject of amusement, scepticism, even ridicule. Some people, however, were curious, and wanted to know more.

My practice was busy and so was the demand for lectures. I was now giving at least two public lectures a month, and although I generally confronted a sceptical audience, once I started giving demonstrations and could prove to people that their feet were virtually the barometers of their health and could reflect their inner selves, I always left behind me a converted audience. People were absolutely amazed when I found a sensitivity in their feet which reflected a neck condition and even more impressed when I could say, 'I think you have suffered an injury or an accident to your neck – there seems to be a lot of congestion and tension in this area'.

'However did you know?' would be the answer. 'I injured my neck in a road accident last year – how on earth can you tell that by my feet?'

I lectured in shabby old wooden huts in the middle of muddy fields for various small ladies' clubs in remote villages, where we all huddled around a tiny electric fire and had to wear our overcoats, but we still managed to create an atmosphere of interest no matter how shabby or remote the venues of the gatherings were. At other grander occasions I would lecture in large luxurious London hotels, where I would be the after-dinner speaker at the annual general meetings of various organisations.

I frequently gave 'cosy chats' at the 'mother and baby meetings' in our local villages, showing mothers how by applying Reflexology to the tiny feet of their children, they could help relieve colic, and other digestive disturbances. These meetings were always great fun and young mothers, in particular, were so enthusiastic and appreciated how they could give some help to their families even with the very limited knowledge that they gained from these get-togethers.

My brother, Tony, was equally busy in his London practice. He was and still is an excellent therapist and had a great following in his part of the world.

Richard believed in my work, for he had benefited himself from its effect on his health. He told people at work about Reflexology and the great benefit it had had on Jonathan and about the many other successes I was achieving.

However, the strain of the emotional tensions in my life took its toll on my health, and I broke out in severe attacks of eczema all over my body, including my face and eyes. I was just one red, itchy, scaly mass and was hardly recognisable. To Richard this was just a reaction to some external irritant: detergent, powder or something similar. He could not, or would not, recognise this as a desperate cry for help, a sign of extreme frustration, a warning of mental breakdown.

Clutching at straws, I saved up enough from the money I earned in my practice for us to have a short holiday in Holland, the first break we had had abroad since our marriage. It was enjoyable while we were away, but when we returned Richard retreated into one of his sulking silences, over what I never did find out. As far as I was concerned everything was spoilt, it was all destroyed for me, the effort of saving, planning, the excitement of travelling abroad by ourselves that I had thought and hoped would give some new vitality to our marriage.

We really did have everything, everything that mattered, a lovely family, a comfortable home, sufficient money now to make ends meet with a bit left over, but things were still far from being right.

I tried desperately to keep the peace, to share out the attention and affection equally among everybody. Maybe I did not make a very good job of it, but I did try. I did my best. I did my best to accept his moods, his retreats into periods of silence which we all dreaded, when there would be a total lack of communication and tension all round. I never could understand how retreating into a shell solves any problems there may have been, and as unfortunately I was not a thought-reader I was never able to guess what was wrong and put it right.

He was such a support on the practical side of our life. I never knew what it was for a repair not to be done almost immediately, our house was perfectly decorated and he was hard-working and very supportive of my physical disability, but it just was not enough. I would rather have had a scruffier home and a happier atmosphere.

The painful, horrific spread of my eczema brought home to me just how powerful was the influence of the mind on the body, proved how unhappiness, tension and frustration all take their toll and I imagined how physically ill I would have been if all this inflammation on my skin had been directed inwards, and perhaps had attacked a vital organ or function. Even the medical profession accept that disease or at least 75 per cent of it is induced by stress. After this experience I would say that more like 90 per cent of illness today is triggered by emotional situations, and I also know that the mind is the greatest controlling influence in our body. Our thought patterns, our reactions to situations, powerful negative reactions directed at individuals, all in turn have a negative effect on our body.

There is, in life, an indefinable law of cause and effect; as within, so without, and this I firmly believe.

I longed to be able to pour out my heart to Richard, and I should have been able to, but if I am honest with myself, I was frightened of his reaction to situations and unfortunately fear destroys trust. I believe that marriage is the closest, most intimate relationship there is, and surely, if your bodies can become united, then you should be able to 'open your soul' to the person with whom you share your life. I constantly found him unapproachable.

My eczema continued to worsen. Most nights I spent hours under a cold shower trying desperately to find some relief, and eventually I went to a skin specialist. I remember that consultation. Richard sat in the room reading the newspaper as though he wanted to detach himself totally from the situation. The specialist said that I was 'in a deplorable condition' and needed immediate admission into St John's Skin Hospital; the treatment would be hydrocortisone by mouth and hydrocortisone skin wraps and I would need to be admitted for at least three weeks. As we drove home I knew in my heart first, that I was not going to leave my family for three weeks, and second, that the drugs might well heal my skin temporarily, but unfortunately they would not give me that 'inner peace' that I needed. So I declined the offer of admission and consulted a medical herbalist, who treated the cause, my mental state, and this treatment helped a little.

This was the most miserable period of my whole life, far worse than John's death, worse than anything I had experienced before, because I could not see any way out.

One morning, the turning-point of my life, I looked into the mirror at my ugly red scaly face. My skin looked rather like crocodile hide, my eyes were red and swollen. I asked myself out loud, 'Why are you, Ann Gillanders, putting up with this miserable existence with a man you cannot understand and who is just as unhappy as you are?' I was sure that he wanted the marriage to end. It was obvious that life with me and the family was intolerable for him.

I don't doubt that Richard suffered at this time too, for nothing is ever totally one-sided, but nor do marriages always break up on a 50–50 basis; the load need not be evenly distributed. Ill as I felt, instead of being complacent and timid, I became angry with him and I firmly defended my children. I was all they had and no longer were they going to lead a life of unhappiness with a broken mother. Our whole problem was lack of communication, we never did come to a solution over this and yet I can honestly say that he is the only person that I have been unable to communicate with.

My respect for him had gone, I stopped slotting into the space that he wanted me to fit into, I told him in no unrestricted terms just what I felt about him. Richard went away to Scotland for Christmas. He was away for a week and peace returned to our home, the hostility had vanished, the tensions had gone, and we could all breathe again.

Richard returned for the new year. Things were just as bad as before, and then one night there was a terrible explosion of anger and that was the end of our marriage. As soon as we had separated, he wanted us to get together and 'talk about the situation'. The talking should have been done years ago, now it was too late, and despite all his pleadings to return, I knew that I could never be what he wanted me to be. A life with him would be plagued with restrictions and conditions, and that I would never accept.

My grandmother used to say, 'Leopards never change their spots, but sometimes they are clever enough to whitewash them over for convenience, that is all right until the rain comes!' How right she was, people don't change, and after all, if they are happy with the way they are, why should they?

16 A career in teaching

It is never easy to sever a marriage, no matter how miserable you have been or how justified you feel in the action that you are taking. It is so easy to make up your mind, but it is so difficult to make up your heart. I was plagued with guilt, mainly guilt in denying Heather a father. My other children had been denied one through death, now this child was going to be without her father through my decision. Richard was desperate to come back to us, to try again, but I could not cope with any more tension, I did not deserve it and I certainly was not going to sacrifice my peace of mind ever again. Never again was I going to live a repressive existence with anybody. Very slowly, after weeks and weeks of a muddled mind and a foggy depression that seemed to engulf me, I started to emerge into life again and, hallelujah, my eczema started to disappear. First it healed from my thighs and feet, next my hands which had been so severely cracked and painful, and lastly my face healed and the swelling around my eyes reduced. Within a month of our separation my skin was perfect again – almost a miracle after 18 months of torture. I felt like a bottle of champagne with the cork removed.

Throughout those long difficult weeks of readjustment, of healing or contemplation patients continued to come for Reflexology. It was just as well as I had no other form of income at that time, and apart from the mortgage and rates being paid all other bills were my responsibility. I remember one financial crisis when my Mini had to go into the garage for a major repair and the bill was twice as much as expected. The Bank Manager helped me over that hurdle.

My practice grew by leaps and bounds. It was quite usual for me to work 9-1 and 2-4 in the afternoon, and then start again at 7 until 10 p.m. Whatever positive spirit there is above, I was definitely guided during those early months. A little voice within me constantly said, 'Don't be afraid, you have so much potential, use it, develop yourself.' In the wee small hours of the morning the other voice was there, the voice that made me feel guilty about parting Heather from her father.

A fighter by nature, I had not 'thrown in the sponge' just on a whim or fancy. I could not go back to the silences, to the moods, to being emotionally deprived. I saw Richard several times during those next few months and several times I nearly changed my mind and had another go. I felt so sorry for him for I knew that unless he changed his attitude to people and dropped his aggressive defences he would be destined to walk a very lonely road.

Every time I returned home after seeing him I revelled in the warm, relaxed, happy atmosphere that now prevailed. The children were contented, there was peace within those walls, and there was no way I would ever give that up, disability or no disability. I had made it before and I would make it again, only this time I was going to stretch myself to my maximum capabilities. I was not going to struggle financially, and my children were going to have every opportunity that I could possibly offer them. These vows I made to myself silently and deliberately with a conviction that made me tremble with anticipation.

There were a number of financial problems to be resolved. Richard was living in a bed-sit, which he was not at all pleased about, but I needed to be able to stay in the bungalow, where the lack of stairs enabled me to be independent. In the meantime, while the solicitors sorted things out, which was obviously going to take months and months, I had to improve my finances to enable me to live anywhere.

My brother Tony and I had talked vaguely about starting to teach Reflexology. We wondered if we could form a small school as so many of our satisfied patients were expressing a desire to learn so that they in turn could help their friends and families. The idea of teaching appealed particularly to me, as it would also mean that Reflexology would spread all over the country and perhaps the world, and as it was such a wonderful science and so beneficial to mankind it was right that it should be developed for more and more people to benefit from.

We talked at length about it one weekend. We decided we would call our school Zone Therapy Tutorials and Development and placed a very small advertisement in a health magazine: 'Zone Therapy Tutorials: Training in Reflexology commencing in April 1981'. Tony and I worked on a programme of training and then hired a small conference room in a local hotel. Within two months 12 people had booked into our course, to our delight. Together we taught the history, development and application of foot Reflexology. Our courses became more and more successful and over the next year grew into much larger classes. The students were happy, they learned with the same enthusiasm as we both had for our work. Now, too, we had money in the bank, the financial stresses had gone, and for the first time in my life I could buy things without worrying about paying the bills each month.

Jenny was one of my first students at our courses in Reflexology; steeped in an interest in alternative medicine, the occult and spirituality generally we formed a firm friendship which has lasted many years. She always believed in me, encouraging me to develop my abilities. She is a very genuine person whose friendship I value deeply.

The bungalow where we lived was in an extremely delightful setting with lovely gardens. Surrounded by conifer trees, it really was a haven of peace, and eighteen months after we had separated the bungalow was awarded to me in the divorce settlement. Now that I knew that I was going to be able to stay there permanently I had many plans to improve and enlarge the accommodation. I first applied for planning permission to convert the garage into a treatment room. I got estimates from builders and then saved hard with some help from the bank, to get the £3000 together for the conversion. When the builders had finished it really looked delightful: a proper treatment room for my patients – a far cry from the medical couch in my bedroom that I had been using for these last few years, and so another ambition was realised.

I was now living the life that I had longed for over the years. I was able to keep an ever-open door for my friends and also those of my children – something we had missed out on for a long time. Everyone's self-confidence increased and I was beginning to believe in myself again. My children were all doing extremely well. They were fine, intelligent young people who I knew would succeed in whatever career they chose. Mark had obtained his ONC in Chemistry, Physics and Maths and had a job as a technician in a chemical company. Clare had started work as a secretary in an estate agents, so there were just Heather and Jonathan at school. Heather was nearly nine at this time and Jonathan was at a very good grammar school near Cambridge. Heather maintained contact with her father and saw him every Sunday. I encouraged her relationship with him, explaining to her that just because we were divorced and could not live together there was no reason on earth why she could not have a good relationship with him.

Few people ever realise that one goes through a very similar grieving situation during the period of a divorce, as after the death of a partner. In fact, I feel that divorce is even more difficult to accept and cope with than a bereavement. Death is final, there are no decisions to be made and it is far easier for children to accept the death of a parent than to be torn between 'divided loyalties' and to have to be 'shared out' by parents on festive occasions. Having a 'Saturdays-only' father takes a lot of getting used to. Bereavement is more socially acceptable than divorce ever is, and you get little sympathy from friends and relatives when you are going through the trauma of a divorce, whereas the bereaved have the compassion of all.

Tony went back to America, back to the Institute in Florida where he had received his training in Reflexology. He had a good friendship with the Director of the Institute and decided to further his training. When he returned a few weeks later, he was accompanied by Mr Byers, the Director of the Institute of Reflexology. Evidently he had expressed a desire to meet me to discuss the possibility of Tony and me taking on a Directorship of the Institute and becoming responsible for teaching on a much larger scale, not only in England but in other countries as well.

It seemed a golden opportunity, with plenty of prospects attached to it. Although I was sad to give up the little school we had started together and which was doing so well, it was too good to miss. To work for a large international concern would be far easier, and it would be a great challenge really to develop Reflexology throughout the UK. Within a week contracts were drawn up and we had some basic instruction in organising teaching on a much grander scale.

We decided to make London our main venue and three months later held our first class in a posh London hotel. It was a great success, and over the next year the numbers grew. Reflexology was at last really becoming known, with many of our therapists starting their own professional practices. By this time I had a very efficiently run office with a part-time secretary. I also did some of the office work myself, but the school was growing faster than we had ever imagined. Here was a wonderful therapeutic treatment, safe, satisfying and highly effective, that used no drugs, no instruments, no special creams or oils. All that was needed was just a pair of hands that could be trained to work in a very effective way. Hands were meant for healing, and healing means loving and giving of yourself to all who come into your care. Most of the people who sought out Reflexology at that time were those who, as I like to call it, had been 'made redundant' from the National Health Service and had been discharged with the formidable and hopeless statement: 'I am sorry, there is nothing more that can be done for you. You will just have to learn to live with it.' Some people do accept that as their fate, others have a little spark of hope left and look to other forms of relief from their sufferings. This is where alternative medical treatment, such as Reflexology, comes into its own. My life had taken on a real purpose, I was still as fascinated in the results achieved by Reflexology and every sick person who became well increased my confidence in the power of this ancient therapy.

Requests were coming in for us to extend our teaching to the Continent, in particular Switzerland, and in April 1982 we made our début in Geneva.

The language problem was solved by our having an interpreter. My brother, and two other good friends who acted as instructors at the courses accompanied us on our trip. We had to take an enormous amount of equipment with us: projector, slides, students' files, masses of medical books, and books on Reflexology, medical charts and office equipment. It was rather like moving house and on our arrival at London airport we were just surrounded by cases and cases. It did not affect me as I could not carry them in any case, but was quite a physical effort for our helpers, and raised eyebrows at the check-in points when we were charged for excess baggage. 'Whatever have you got in these cases?' said one stewardess, 'Gold nuggets?'

Switzerland was wonderful. I fell in love with Geneva, and always say that if I ever had to live anywhere else I would choose Geneva with its snow-clad mountains, pine trees, and superb cleanliness. It puts our country to shame; people out there really seem to care about their country, there is no vandalism, and very little crime.

Our training courses were supported by large numbers of students. We started off with about 40 in a class and over the next few years the numbers expanded to more than 70, usually with a mixture of about eight nationalities.

Every evening after the class we would go somewhere socially. Students would invite us to their chalets for dinner, and off we would go by taxi to chocolate-box chalets and villas mainly built in solid wood with verandahs, baskets of hanging geraniums, large log-burning stoves, and we would settle down with nine or ten guests at a table to eat the speciality of the canton.

Our interpreter, Madame Faris, was excellent at her job. She spoke three languages fluently and told us wonderful stories of her experiences as an interpreter or as a companion to duchesses and counts all over the world. She had an exuberant personality and was a person whose friendship I valued greatly. Her husband Farid, who was equally charming, had a language school in Switzerland where he taught English. We made three regular trips each year to Geneva and our school became recognised and highly respected.

I was lucky to have a fit, willing mother who came and looked after the family while I was away. We stayed away for short periods only, never more than a week. When I returned it was always with Lindt chocolate, Swiss and French cheeses and little souvenirs from Switzerland.

As our school expanded, the office work became so heavy that my one part-time secretary needed assistance, so I took on another part-timer, a friend of mine, actually the daughter of Joyce who had been my housekeeper for years when the children were small. Jane was now struggling to bring up three boys on her own, so she was glad of the job.

We opened another training establishment in Paris, then Brighton, and later in 1983 expanded yet again and held classes in Manchester. We also used to exhibit at the Alternative Medicine Exhibition which was a superb outlet for the promotion of unorthodox medicines. Here one could sample just about every kind of treatment, from acupuncture to homeopathy, eat a superb range of vegetarian and whole foods, visit the many stalls offering all kinds of herbs and massage oils, and all sorts of exercise machines. Most impressive of all was the lecture theatre where one could listen to a host of lecturers talk on their chosen subject. My brother or I used to lecture here, and the whole four-day event was an exciting and stimulating experience for one and all.

17 Children's progress

During one of my trips to Switzerland I had met a dental surgeon and his wife Maria. They lived in a superb house, ultra-modern, with a futuristic kitchen – never before had I seen so much equipment in a kitchen. Most of the internal walls were marble, and the bedrooms had balconies with breath-taking views. After Maria became a student of ours, we became friends, and we often used to stay with them during our teaching courses in Geneva.

At one side of the house there was a large swimming pool, plus a gymnasium, and in the basement was a fallout shelter. Apparently all new buildings in Switzerland have this amenity. There were also spacious grounds, which is very unusual in Switzerland. It is such a small country that accommodation tends to be built upwards in very high blocks of flats. Very few people are ever able to afford a property of their own as the cost of land is so exorbitant.

Maria wanted an au pair for the coming year, and I wondered if my daughter Clare would like to go for the experience. It would also give her the opportunity to learn French. So in the spring of 1982 Clare went off to Geneva to work for a year. We all went to London Airport to wave her a fond farewell. I think airports are terribly emotional places, and at the last minute Clare almost changed her mind. However, we made it clear that she was to treat it as a holiday, and that if she did not like the household or the work then she could always return home.

We missed her a lot, but I knew that she would love Switzerland as much as I did. Every fortnight I had a long newsy letter; she was making new friends, enjoying a good social life, and going to school twice a week to learn French.

When we went to Geneva in September for a Reflexology training course we were able to spend some time with Clare. She had been on skiing trips with the family and was enjoying it all immensely. Her French was fluent and she had already obtained a diploma from the language school she was attending.

Jonathan's progress in his health had been maintained. At nearly 15 he was a very tall, handsome young man with dark brown hair and even darker brown eyes. He was doing exceedingly well at school and showed ability in many directions. Though he had chosen sciences for his options, he also had creative talent and could paint in oils most beautifully. He had a very positive attitude to life and great confidence in himself. His asthma was now a thing of the past, though he still had a weakness in his chest and if he ever caught cold his wheeziness would return. On other occasions he would have outbreaks of eczema on his hands, but he never had to return to the huge doses of drugs that he had relied on as a small boy; in fact he never had to seek the support of drugs again.

Jonathan had grown up so like his father, not only in looks but in his personality – like John he really thought he was 'quite something'! Jonathan had the same shaped hands as his father with wide fingers and square nails, he was left-handed as John was, and in many of his mannerisms resembled his father exactly, thus proving that even our mannerisms are genetically controlled.

Heather at 10 was a dear little girl, so kind and caring, always involving herself in helping people. She used to worry if ever I was under par or a bit achy or if my back was troubling me. I suppose she looked upon me as her mainstay.

I think that perhaps Heather and I were very similar in nature. We liked the same things, felt the same way about many situations, and I was sure that she would choose a career that involved caring and helping people. Whether it would be nursing or something similar I could not be sure, but Heather belonged in a situation where her natural compassion and concern for humanity could be appreciated.

As a family we had made tremendous progress in the years since my divorce. I had learnt self-evaluation. For too long I had considered myself not worthy of much. Neither my brother nor I had had much praise as children. Although our parents were quite proud of us both, nothing much was ever said, and my disability had brought the feeling of being a second-class citizen, which did not help.

I firmly believe that children need to be loved every day of their lives. Whether they are good or naughty, whether they be boys or girls, they should have loving, expressive contact from both parents. It's not cissy to kiss and cuddle a boy – the Continentals do it all the time. Criticism should be constructive and kept to a minimum; the best way to undermine any child's confidence is to bring him or her up in an environment of harsh criticism, over-strict discipline and little opportunity for self-expression.

If I could bring up my children all over again I would increase the amount of affection that I displayed to them all, as I now know that children who are really loved and who are brought up to believe that they are 'special' grow up into mature, confident adults who repeat exactly the same process in raising their children and get exactly the same results.

Children who are the victims of homes where there is a lot of tension and fear, over-strict discipline and a cold and repressive atmosphere never develop emotionally. They usually remain as 'immature children' for life, finding it hard to commit themselves to anything or anybody and normally form very inadequate relationships. If they have children they tend to repeat the whole miserable pattern again.

I am sure my children suffered from my broken marriage and all the miseries and tensions leading up to that event, but all I could do was to provide a happy, warm, loving atmosphere. Our home now had an ever-open door, we often had friends staying for the weekends, lots of parties. The children knew that they could always bring a friend back for an unexpected meal – there was always plenty. It was far better that they should bring their friends home than to wander about the town getting into trouble. Instead of criticising them unduly, I tried to set certain standards and an example of how one has to get up and go on whatever problems and difficulties present themselves.

My financial position was now very comfortable, and therefore I intended doing everything possible to encourage my children in whatever careers they decided upon. I was able to have private tutors for them all once a week to help with any weaknesses they had. Above all, I wanted them to set their sights high and to enter a working career that gave them real satisfaction. I hoped that Jonathan would go on to university or college or whatever area of education he chose. I knew he had quite extraordinary talents in so many directions and was determined to encourage him every inch of the way.

Clare's 21st birthday in 1984 was another happy occasion. We hired a hall and gave a big party to which all her friends came. She had done extremely well in her job in estate agency and had now become a negotiator and took on a lot of responsibility, which suited her as she was a born organiser and excellent at management.

Clare went into a flat with a girlfriend soon after her birthday. They decided to buy one on a joint mortgage so as to get a 'foot on the ladder', in the property market and have an accumulating asset for the future. I missed her a lot in the first few weeks but saw her very frequently and was delighted at the work they put into their flat. After only a few months it looked like a little palace, and it certainly meant that when she decided to get married there would be a lump sum from the sale of the flat to put down on a house.

She had had several boyfriends over the years, but as soon as I met John I knew at once that he was to be 'special'. He was the most relaxed, amiable person that I have ever met, and I was delighted when they announced their engagement in the spring of 1985. John was the second son in a family of four; he had an elder brother and a younger brother and sister who were twins. They seemed a happy family, and I liked his mother and father.

18 Israel

Israel now beckoned us. The Israelis had heard about Reflexology from one of our Israeli students, Schmulic Rosen, who had come to England to join our training courses. 'Come to Israel and teach there,' he said. 'There is so much interest in Reflexology and a place for you both. I will act as your agent and get together sufficient students to establish a training school.'

And so in May 1982 we made our first trip to Israel, taking with us a great friend and excellent therapist, Philip Lowe, who had worked with us on our courses in London. We left Heathrow wearing jackets but when we landed at the Ben-Gurion Airport in Israel it was just like stepping into a sauna, the heat was so intense, and this was supposed to be their cool season! We were met by Schmulic and his wife and drove at great speed past miles of cacti, huge bushes of lemon-scented verbena, and everywhere there seemed to be an enormous amount of new building going on.

After an hour, we arrived at Hertzlia and our motel, which was very pleasantly laid out in beautiful gardens with a large fish pond and an abundance of blossom in the most vivid colours, enormous scarlet geraniums, azaleas and a mass of brilliantly coloured trailing plants growing along the brick walls that were unfamiliar to me. The motel was owned by an Israeli and his American wife, charming people who made us feel so welcome and at home.

The bedrooms were typically tropical with pale blue marble floors and walls to match, wooden beds, a mosquito net if you needed it and a simple shower room and toilet. Hot water was free as each motel unit had its own supply heated by solar panels, but the cold water used for watering the beautiful gardens which had to be attended to twice a day was very expensive. Each house had a water meter and you had to pay heavily to use the supply.

The dining room was attractively laid out with circular tables and chairs, rush matting on the floors and lots of exotic tapestries on the walls. After unpacking our belongings and getting organised for the training course the following day, we sat out on the balcony and watched the antics of a vivid blue kingfisher as he swooped upon the fish in the pond and devoured several at great speed. We watched lizards darting about and were warned about the possibility of small snakes, but in fact we never saw any. The perfume from the verbena was overpowering, and as we sipped iced cold lager, it was like living in a totally different world, hard to believe that 12 hours previously we had been in London.

One minute it seemed to be light and then within half an hour we were plunged into pitch blackness, as there is very little twilight. The Israeli and his American wife started work very early in the morning. Around 5 we would become aware of them being up and about and could hear the faint noise of the water sprinklers. The gardener came in at that time too and many tradesmen seem to deliver goods at around 5 or 6 in the morning.

We sat out on the verandah in the morning and had breakfast which consisted of enormous tomatoes, as luscious to eat as any fruit, small cucumbers which were sweet and had the flavour and texture of melon and cucumber, a large variety of different breads, goats' milk yogurt and cheese and a rather salty type of salami which was obviously extremely popular with the natives but which we were not very keen on.

We held our first training course in the Art of Movement Centre in Hertzlia, where classes for yoga, dance, gymnastics and so on were held. It was some way out in a very barren, desert-like area. We found teaching the Israelis difficult; they were noisy, over-exuberant and inclined to wander off suddenly from the class and talk volubly, so keeping a disciplined class together was very hard going. In fact, it was rather like keeping a flock of sheep together! Nevertheless, they were certainly very enthusiastic and thought that Reflexology was absolutely wonderful.

I found it difficult to cope with the intense heat. My right leg became very swollen and painful, and standing for hours in the training courses while we lectured and gave practical instruction to the students did not help. I relied on my brother to do most of the walking about at that course and decided that, much as I enjoyed Israel, the northern climate certainly suited me and my leg better when it came to walking. Although winters in England caused me to have a blue frozen limb, somehow it is easier to warm something up than cool it down.

Israel is unique, a country of great atmosphere and steeped in history. The people too are very different. It certainly is not a peaceful or restful country and I found it alarming to see armed police everywhere. There is a lot of noise and tension, and the driving is absolutely mad. All day long all you hear in the town is the loud honking of car horns and non-stop hustle and bustle. Far off in the distance we could hear gunfire and the rumble of bombs. The Israelis took all this as quite normal in their country and seemed hardly to notice it, but we all found it disturbing, to say the least.

We went by bus to a neighbouring town. What an experience – you practically take your life in your hands. There seems to be no control on numbers, everybody piles in and as soon as the seats are filled then the aisles become crammed with people squashed together like sardines in a tin, shopping bags are dumped on the floors and it is quite common to find a bag full of 50 oranges right in front of your seat or an enormous water melon and perhaps a parrot in a cage just to add to the confusion. The bus drivers drive alarmingly fast, blasting on their horns all the time and when somebody wants to get off at a stop – well, it would make a comedy film. It is quite usual for 20 to have to get out of the bus to allow just one to get off, and then they all pile in again, people, parrots, goods and all.

We were quite appalled at the very poor hygiene in the shops. Meat hangs up on hooks and is covered with flies, but nobody seems to worry much about it. Pâtisseries have shelves of gâteaux and bread all exposed to the heat and flies, and there are many open snack bars along the pavements with no attention to hygiene at all. Very little food is properly covered anywhere, apart from in the large supermarkets which are obviously properly refrigerated and protected. Yet everyone seems to survive.

Schmulic Rosen and his wife made us very welcome at their home in the evenings and we met their two sons and daughter. All Israeli youngsters, male and female, have to serve two years in the army, similar to our National Service in the past. We ate the most superb Chinese food that we had ever tasted at their home and had some truly memorable evenings with them during our trip, meeting many of their friends and family.

There was a four-day gap between our training course in Hertzlia and the second one which was to be held in Jerusalem, and so we spent these four days sight-seeing. We visited the Garden of Gethsemane. There is certainly something very special about it, although it was spoiled by the rather cheap wooden souvenirs, crosses, camels, statues, cards and so on. When we went into the shrine erected there we felt its unique atmosphere reminding us of what had taken place there so long ago.

We paid a visit to Jaffa and Java, then on to Bethelehem where we saw the birth-place of Christ – a very unimpressive shrine. We spent a day in Jerusalem, visiting the old part first. In the enormous market place where all the natives bring their wares, men and women sit on the steps that wind through the city and furious bargaining takes place. You can buy just about anything from a bag of fresh dates to good quality leather.

I was surprised to see a woman walk through the market with a huge basket of fruit balanced upon her head and a bundle of rags under her arm. She found a spot on one of the steps and settled herself down, placing her basket of fruit on the ground in front of her and the bundle of rags behind. I went up to her and bought some of her fruit and was astonished to find that the bundle of rags was a very new baby. She just put it behind her on the steps in a basket, feeding it when necessary, and there she and the baby stayed until all her goods had been sold. Then up she got, empty basket in one hand and baby under her arm, and strolled through the market and disappeared from view. I was told by our Israeli friends that this was quite common practice!

Leaving the hospitality of our friends who owned the motel, we made our way to what we would call the YMCA in England, a very large hostel for young people with a large conference hall on the ground floor which was used frequently for meetings. This was where we held our second training course, right in the centre of Jerusalem. Somehow it seemed the right place to teach an ancient therapy such as Reflexology. Again the course was well attended and the students were full of enthusiasm, keen to learn, keen for us to return in order that they might learn more and encourage their friends to come along and study this fascinating science.

We still had two days of sight-seeing before we returned to England at the end of May, so back we went to Jerusalem and visited the Wailing Wall. The Israelis do actually place pieces of paper in the wall with messages to loved ones who have passed on. Then they roll these pieces of paper into a small tube and wedge them between the bricks in the wall, and start wailing or praying to God to deliver their messages. They also wail at the wall for days when a member of the family dies. We visited the Golden Dome, and Schmulic took us to many of the old buildings of historical interest.

I wanted to see the Dead Sea before going home, and the following day set off in Schmulic's old car. The route that we took was right off the beaten track, and we went through very primitive villages where the women still do all the hard physical work. There they are carrying water urns on their heads, working in the fields, while the men sit on the steps of the houses talking and smoking enormous long pipes. Children are also frequently seen doing quite heavy work in the fields.

As we drove along the roads we would see small boys displaying oranges, lemons and water melons untidily arranged on a board raised from the pavement with a few bricks, bargaining with local people and tourists.

Scattered here and there in the outskirts of the most primitive villages were very rough huts which were still inhabited. They were made up of rough wood and cardboard and hardly looked strong enough to stand, let alone be lived in. Outside the hut an old couple would sit over a small fire over which a pot was suspended which was obviously their only means of cooking. A mangy-looking donkey and a few chickens were their only possessions. They were able to survive in these very primitive conditions only because of the constant warm climate. In a different environment they would have died long ago.

There is quite a selection of different religious sects in Israel, all living in their own communities quite separate from others. It is possible to identify these various religions by each house in the community having a bright blue-stained coloured glass in one side of the building. It was very striking as we drove by to see the sun reflecting on this vivid bright blue which certainly could not be missed. In another community which was set high on a hill the glass was a brilliant green.

On our last evening in Jerusalem a shy young Israeli couple called at the hostel asking to see the lady from England who could 'heal through the feet'. They had brought their baby who was about 15 months old and severely spastic, in the hopes that Reflexology might be able to do something for him. The young woman spoke no English at all, but the husband was able to converse quite well. I tried to explain as best I could that although this therapy is wonderful it cannot reverse damage sustained at birth. They then asked me if I would like to visit the kibbutz where they lived, and so off I went with them. They were obviously proud to show me around the area, and the strong community life was very dominant there. Most people seemed quite happy living in these kibbutzim and I found the atmosphere there quite peaceful, so different from the hurly-burly of life in the major large towns.

It was a most memorable trip which I would not have missed for the world, but I was pleased to return to England with all its lush greenery, and it was great to feel a cool breeze once again instead of the intense heat which beat down out of a cloudless blue sky day after day.

I started to write articles for many well-known magazines. Reflexology was at last becoming known, and now when I tried to introduce its benefits to a stranger, instead of looking puzzled many said that they had 'heard about it from a friend' who had found it gave great relief in easing a back condition; others thought they had 'read about it somewhere'. Gradually an interest was dawning in alternative or complementary medicine, which were beginning to be used and accepted instead of being regarded with suspicion as 'witchcraft' or spiritualism.

I always refer to all such medicine as 'medicine of the soul'. After all, herbalism, homeopathy, acupuncture, and naturopathic approaches to disease have all been here from the beginning of time. Surely the orthodox approach to medicine is the 'alternative' one? Drugs and all the mechanical devices used in treating disease plus the increased use of sophisticated surgery are all very recent; in fact it is only since the war that orthodox medicine has advanced to the level that it has reached today. I once gave a lecture to a large group of retired GPs many of whom were in their eighties, so they had doctored at a time when there were very few drugs to aid suffering, and the bedside manner and basic commonsense approaches to sickness had to be relied upon. After I had finished my lecture which they were all extremely interested in, the chairman of the group (also a doctor) thanked me for coming and ended the meeting by saying, 'If all the drugs were hurled into the sea, it would be a wonderful day for mankind but a very sad one for the fishes!'

We returned to Israel a year later, and this time three of my children went with me, Clare, Jonathan and Heather. As there were so many of us, this time we stayed in a large air-conditioned flat in Hertzlia. We were on the seventh floor and were able to enjoy the benefits of the large swimming pool which was so warm that it was like being in a hot bath.

The children revelled in the warmth and found Israel as fascinating as we had done on our first visit. Young Heather who was only 9 at the time suffered badly from sunburn. In the half-hour that it took us to unpack our cases, she had gone into the pool, and just exposing her shoulders above the water level for that short time caused quite severe burning. She was quite poorly for a couple of days, and after the experience she always wore a cotton tee shirt over her costume and went in the water only for short dips. We all stayed in our flat during the heat of the day as even the pavements were too hot to walk on at mid-day – you could even feel the heat through sandals!

The Reflexology courses were as popular as ever, well attended, and a lot of general interest was shown in the country as a whole.

We did have one hair-raising experience. Two of the students with whom we had become very friendly invited us to visit them for a weekend. Their home was in Galilee and to reach them meant a three-hour bus ride. When we went down to the bus station, we found that the bus fare for the four of us was so enormous that it would have taken nearly all of our money. As I was not feeling too well with an upset stomach, we decided to change our plans and returned to the flat.

Later that day a bomb exploded in the village where we were going and caused a lot of severe damage. Fortunately nobody was killed or injured in the house where we would have stayed, but the whole area was closed off and nobody was let in or out for over 10 days, so it was certainly a very lucky escape for us.

19 My people

Meeting the wonderful people whom I have treated in these past years has been, and I hope will be for many years yet a memorable experience and one that I feel honoured to have been chosen to share. To have helped so many sick and suffering people, to experience the faith that they have shown in me has been awe-inspiring. I have shared in their joys and sorrows, and today am treating the children of young people who came to me many years ago for treatment.

I want to share with you now some of the humorous and sad situations in which I have been involved thanks to my work as a reflexologist.

The first to spring to mind was an Australian woman who had been reared on a sheep farm. She had married a very eccentric aristocratic Englishman who seemed to have a strange life-style. They had four girls and lived in a large Victorian house way out in the country and kept droves of sheep. The mother was very much the 'earth mother' type. She grew an abundance of fruit and vegetables and seemed to live an extremely tense existence with her eccentric husband, hence her troublesome migraines. She always arrived with an enormous wicker basket in which she seemed to keep everything. She was a large lady, attractive in a natural way, and at one of her routine appointments she hoisted herself in an ungainly fashion upon the medical couch and began to relate the weird behaviour of her eccentric husband and, it seemed, rather neurotic children. Evidently it was a great weight off her rather generous chest just to have somebody to listen to her problems. However, to my amazement, she leaned over the couch, hoisted the enormous wicker basket from the floor and brought out a colander and a carrier bag full of fresh peas which she proceeded to pod at great speed. 'Save me doing them tonight,' she said.

The eccentric husband appeared on the scene during another appointment session. He glided into the consulting room wearing a heavily embroidered kaftan which reached to the floor. On the front and back of the robe were depicted in brilliant orange an enormous snake and two small lizards. He also wore Chinese slippers with upturned toes and strangest of all he carried a large wooden engraved box, and all I could think of as he sat in a chair opposite his wife was that he surely resembled one of the three kings presenting his gifts to the Christ child. It was therefore, in a way, disappointing when he opened his precious box almost with reverence and proceeded to take out one copy of *The Times*, a wallet and a pair of half-rimmed spectacles. His wife made no reaction to the situation whatsoever except to remark that he often acted 'strangely' when he was in the process of another 'invention' (he was in fact a scientist).

I did, however, rid his wife of her migraines.

On another occasion I was asked to treat a large Arabic family in Hampstead, north London – plus the staff of the very large property development company they owned. I was not sure what to expect when after 1½ hours in heavy traffic I came to the most enormous bungalow I had ever seen. Two Rolls-Royces were parked in the drive and eventually the door was opened and in I went to another world, a world of such wealth that it was almost crude and brash. The inner hall was in solid marble with tall pillars to the ceiling and an equally enormous sunken swimming pool with a large selection of palm trees and sun beds scattered along its edges plus large bamboo fans that were electrically controlled to wave delicately at regular intervals.

The head of the family appeared. Clad in a flowing white gown, he was a tense abrupt man who seemed to have no movement at all in his neck, so that in order to turn from right to left or left to right he had to turn his entire body. This was the obvious problem that I had been summoned to treat. I was shown into the master bedroom which had such a thick carpet that it was like trying to walk on soft sand – your feet actually disappeared from view. I treated the father. He seemed such a sick, miserable man who had suffered for years with an arthritic neck. He had been everywhere in the world and had taken every new and magical drug that came on to the market with no success and so Reflexology was his last resort. I gave him the usual 45-minute treatment and then proceeded to give his neck and spine some massage. He seemed physically relieved but made absolutely no comment.

The next patient was one of his eight daughters who had had unending bowel problems, although she was only 24. She had been diagnosed as having diverticulitis and suffered frequent episodes of severe pain. Here was another sad, lonely, dissatisfied person who confided to me that her only purpose in life was to produce as many children as possible for her husband whom in any case she did not love. At 24 she already had four children and was likely to have at least another five. 'My life,' she said, 'has no purpose, just riches and children. There is nothing in life that I cannot buy, only I don't know what I want to give me happiness. I am just a prisoner.'

The third patient in the family was another young daughter, only 17, who was awaiting an arranged marriage within a couple of months to a husband whom she had never met. Her life at the present time was totally given over to buying her trousseau and arranging the enormous wedding for some 800 guests. After the marriage she would start a new life in Saudi Arabia. She suffered severe migraines and seemed to me another frustrated, trapped young woman who had to abide by family traditions and expectations whether she liked them or not.

I spent the whole day there treating the mother, a couple of the sons-in-law, the company secretary. There was not one person among those I treated who seemed to have any inner peace. This was a great lesson to me in proving that money does not bring happiness and, most important of all, it does not give one peace of mind.

The last 'patient' for me to treat was a small boy of three. He was a beautiful child but his right arm was bent up and very stiff; in fact he was unable to use it at all. Evidently there had been some brain damage at birth and although he was not affected in any other way this disabled right arm was the result. I asked if he was having regular hospital treatment or whether there was any possibility of surgery being performed to release the tension in his arm. The father of the child said that they were not in agreement with any surgery as in their religion any birth deformity must be accepted as 'the will of God'. So this lovely child was destined to have a useless right arm and by the time he would be old enough to make his own decisions, it would be far too late. I felt that this was absolutely criminal.

I returned to the Arabic family several times, but eventually the number of people added to the list of treatment grew so much that they asked me to attend twice a week. They also pressed me to go to Saudi Arabia to treat their family and business acquaintances out there. This way of life was not for me. To me there was a vulgarity about so much wealth. Certainly it was a lifestyle that I would never envy. I had no interest in treating those who were so rich that any treatment in the world was available to them just by lifting a telephone and demanding that whoever was required come to them immediately. I wanted to treat ordinary, everyday people, the local country folk, those who really needed me.

Rosie was a beautiful old lady who lived in a small cottage in a nearby village. She was partially sighted and was considerably disabled by arthritis. I started going to her on a regular basis. Her cottage was clean, neat and tidy but it was obvious that money was very short. Her husband had died years earlier and her two beloved sons had been killed in the last war. Rosie had very painful swollen knees which meant that walking was difficult so she spent most of the time indoors. I think her main problem was a broken heart. Photographs of her two handsome sons stood on the mantelpiece and in front of each was a small vase of flowers. An equally attractive picture of a white-haired man, obviously her husband, stood next to those of her sons. I treated Rosie for many months. She was always so upset that I refused to take any fees for treatment. I explained that I did not need it but that she obviously did and that if she just covered the cost of my petrol that would be more than enough. Every week there was a small present, some flowers from her garden, something she had cooked for me. I was always shown photographs of her children when young, pictures of herself as a young woman. She had been blessed with a very happy marriage, having found her 'soulmate', as few ever do. She said she still had a good cry every Christmas and Easter when she got out all the cards and letters from her husband, some of which were so old. She could just manage to read with a magnifying glass.

Rosie related to me such wonderful tales of her life in Essex where she had been born and bred. Her husband had been the village baker and she described their routine of getting up at three in the morning to start lighting the coal ovens and how they baked for hours and hours during the early hours in order to have sufficient supplies for the villages. 'My Len and me had such a time,' she would say. 'We would sit side by side on two wooden crates with a wind-up gramophone, with a bottle of something to pass the time. While the bread was baking we would be singing all the old songs at the tops of our voices. He was a real lad, my Len – every time I bent down to get the bread out of the low oven he would pinch my backside. They were wonderful times, up to your neck in flour next to my Len, flour on your clothes, in your eyes, in your hair.'

Rosie did obtain some good relief with her arthritic knees, but I think I helped more to mend her broken heart. She would be watching out of the window for my car, just like a young child waiting anxiously for its mother to return, and as soon as I was inside she would always say, 'Why does somebody like you have to have a poor old leg like that?' She always called me her 'lady of light' and when I asked her why she called me this, she said, 'You bring so much love and light to my life.'

I went to Rosie's funeral. She was 89 when she died, and was laid to rest alongside her beloved Len. A wonderful lady and friend.

Although I really only ever intended to treat people, circumstances arose one day which might have made me decide to alter my course of direction!

Late one winter's evening I had a telephone call. A very old, weak voice asked me if I could possibly come and visit 'Harold', who was in extreme pain with his back and could hardly move. Mrs Vines had heard of my work from a friend in a neighbouring village and understood that the treatment I gave was excellent for back conditions. 'Please come just as soon as possible,' she said, 'as this is really urgent.' I took brief directions and arranged to visit the following afternoon at 4 o'clock. On approaching the village I eventually found the house which was at the end of a long drive and as I approached the house, which was eerie to say the least, my impulse was to turn around and go back the way I had come. The drainpipes were tied up with old stockings, the letter box had fallen off, all the windows were rotted to pieces and the garden was overgrown like a jungle.

However, Mrs Vines had seen me coming and came out to meet me, a poor, wizened old woman with a hunchback. She was decidedly dirty and was just as unkempt as the house. Another figure appeared round the door – her sister, she said – a small, nervous old woman who was equally dishevelled. 'We'll go round the back way to see Harold,' she said. I thought this was strange but followed her round through a broken-down back gate and into a small cobbled yard. There in front of me was a magnificent black horse. 'Harold' was a horse with a spinal injury.

I gave Mrs Vines a quick explanation that I could not treat animals and got out of that eerie house and strange set-up just as soon as possible. I often wonder how those two old women came to have a horse like that. In no way could they have looked after it and certainly they could never have ridden it. That was a mystery that remains unanswered.

Through my work I met a fine farming family who will always have a special place in my heart. They lived far out in Much Hadham, a lovely Essex village, in one of those farms where the approach to the farmhouse is up a drive about a mile long. Then you enter another world, acres and acres of fields, barns, lovely old farm machinery, and a mass of old shrubs and trees. One of the oak trees which stood majestically on their land was the largest oak tree in Essex.

Walking into the old kitchen was like going back a hundred years. A large Aga stood in one corner, then a coke boiler set back in a recess with a wooden holder in which stood a line of shotguns all in their leather sheaths, a quarry-tiled floor, large butler sink and the most enormous kitchen table. Two comfortable armchairs were placed in front of the boiler. All the modern devices were installed – dishwasher, automatic washing machine, electric mixer – but the kitchen had the added comfort of being a restful place as well as an area that was a hive of activity.

Ann and Maurice had two fine handsome sons, Rodney and Richard. Rodney worked the farm with his elderly father. Although he had been to Oxford and had a degree in English, he much preferred to work in the farming environment. When I met the family Richard was away at university and did not have the same interest in the farm as his brother. A mile away from the farmhouse was a small bungalow in which an elderly aunt lived. Several elderly relatives seemed to have lived there, died and left a space for another elderly relative to move in, and so it went on.

The whole family seemed very supportive of each other and the 'elderlies' had such a lot of care and attention. Nothing seemed too much trouble. It was the caring in that family that attracted and impressed me. There was always a warm welcome. Ann would insist you tried some of her home-cooked ham – I never have tasted ham like it – or would bring to the table a selection of her superb homemade cakes.

Maurice was elderly by the time I met him and had a number of health problems, in particular quite extensive arthritis in his shoulders and hips which made arm movements very difficult. His walking was limited, and he also had a prostate condition.

I treated him with Reflexology for many months and he gained so much benefit from it that he was able to cope with tackling some hedging and cut down a large area of hedges that had become totally overgrown. Reflexology seemed to give him a new lease of life, his mobility increased and he was able to get on and off his beloved tractor with ease. I seemed to treat most of the family for various conditions over the years. Even the sons had the occasional back condition.

In the summer of 1979 I had a call from one of the sons to say that his father had had a stroke, was paralysed down one side and had lost his speech. For such a caring family there was no question of Maurice being taken to hospital, they all preferred to nurse him at home. I was asked if I could possibly come and treat him daily as they were all so sure that Reflexology could help. Every morning for many weeks the elder son, Rodney, picked me up early in the morning and off I went to the farm to treat Maurice. The old man had such faith in me that it was embarrassing. I just hoped I could do some good. I treated Maurice for weeks and he did recover both movement and his speech very rapidly, much to the amazement of the doctor who I think feared the worst. Although the doctor had no idea of how Reflexology worked he actually said, 'It does seem to have done a lot of good, heaven knows how it works, but keep on treating him,' so I did. I had a great affection for Maurice. He was such a lovely old man and it was so rewarding when he got back on his tractor and started to work the farm again, just eight weeks after his stroke. Although I am sure Reflexology helped, he was surrounded with so much tender loving care that I am convinced this played a major part in his recovery.

Apart from my ministrations as a therapist I had some delightful social occasions with this family. One Christmas time I spent an evening with them in their 'Christmas room'. This was a permanent Christmas room with holly and mistletoe entwined around the lovely old beams, a huge Christmas tree, an enormous log fire in the inglenook fireplace, mulled wine, and that very special smell that one gets in very old houses. I loved going there, as it was such an escape from the hurly-burly of modern living.

Maurice lived for many years after his stroke, eventually dying of kidney failure at the age of 82.

Most people go to their local market place just to buy goods, but not so for me. I always referred to my friends the market traders as my 'publicity officers'. Over the years I have treated dozens of the market traders and their families and friends for a wide selection of aches and pains. They have also referred many of their customers to me for their health problems.

A lot of market traders seem to suffer from back troubles caused by lifting all the heavy weights which their job entails.

As I make my twice-weekly trip to the market I almost feel as if I am doing a ward round as I talk to all my 'patients' about the state of their health.

Another of my satisfied patients who springs to mind was a comparatively young man who had very advanced arthritis. His hips and shoulders were severely affected, mobility was limited and he suffered considerable pain.

I was very recently qualified when I first treated Michael and in my enthusiasm to do as much for this poor man as I possibly could, I gave him a lengthy treatment, too long in fact, probably working on the surmise that four teaspoons of medicine gets you better faster than one. This is not in fact so.

The day after his first treatment I had a telephone call from his wife to say that Michael was very unwell. He had severe pain all over his body, had been feverish all night and had diarrhoea. What had I done to him, surely this Reflexology had made his condition worse than ever before?

I assured his good lady that in some cases Reflexology did give quite severe reactions and although this was unpleasant for the patient it was an excellent sign that the body was getting rid of all its impurities. If Michael could just weather the storm and have confidence in what I was saying, I was sure that he would feel so much better in a couple of days.

When I telephoned the second day to ask how he was, the feverish condition still persisted, and he still had severe pain in all his joints but felt slightly better than the day before. On the third day, however, the feverish condition had passed, the pain in his joints had subsided and as he got out of bed he realised that he could move with a freedom that he had lost years ago. There was little pain in his hips, and, miracle upon miracles, he could raise his arms above his head! He rang me to tell me this wonderful news. 'Come again for a treatment,' I said, 'come this evening if you can manage it,' and he came. This time he experienced only a slight reaction.

Week after week Michael returned. Now there was a certain sort of light in his face that was not there before. He looked so much younger. 'I feel better than I have felt in 10 years,' he told me. 'That was when this wretched condition started.' Then it all came out. He had a very unhappy marriage with a tense, cold, uptight woman who was really only interested in her home which was kept like a show house all the time. 'I'm afraid to move in my own home,' he said. 'If I have a bath she can't wait to get in there after me to see if the towels are hung up exactly in order and to make sure that the bath shines as much as it did before. The tension in our marriage is indescribable,' he said. 'I have just been too ill to fight back and try to change things. We should have divorced years ago.'

'You do realise that all this tension and atmosphere is why you have suffered all these years, don't you?' I said.

'I felt sure that my marriage had to be at the bottom of it,' he confessed.

After I had treated Michael on a weekly basis for three months, he had made a wonderful improvement. So I suggested that he cease regular treatment and contact me only if he felt he needed more help.

Three months later I saw Michael in the town arm-in-arm with a very pretty plump woman (not his wife). Holding on to his hand was a small boy and another even younger child was holding hers. Michael was dressed in an old pair of jeans and baggy jumper and wore a pair of old trainers. He was upright and there seemed no evidence of any arthritis anywhere in his body. He looked so happy and relaxed, quite different from the tense, uptight, unhappy man I had first met a year ago. I later heard that he had left his wife and was living with this young woman and her two children. He described his feelings as 'I have been reborn'. Here was a situation where Reflexology certainly changed the entire direction of someone's life in rather a drastic way.

I have been privileged to treat people of all races and creeds, they have come to me in their chauffeur-driven Rolls-Royces or on their ancient bikes; they have all suffered health problems, they all had their emotional stresses, be it family or business and they were all seeking relief. Whatever their status, none of them was exempt from suffering, and they all had to learn that health could not be bought and that inner peace could not be obtained by paying cash down.

20 Unsettled

My career in Reflexology answered all my dreams as far as ambition was concerned, but I was unsettled in that I did not like some of the elements involved in working for a large commercial American concern. I felt that more involvement in the true humanitarian aspect of healing should dominate a school involved in the training of therapists to work in an area of health care that needed such an abundance of compassion. Most people sought out Reflexology as a last resort and had been suffering for years. Many of the patients who received such an improvement in their health through Reflexology went into training and became first-class therapists.

I wanted to write a book on Reflexology. I had so much experience in these last years, but knew that a book written by me would not be very favourably received on the American side. I wanted to produce a quarterly magazine for the reflexologist, *Healing Points*. I knew I could do it, but again there would have been a very adverse reaction from America.

On the practical side, standing for hours lecturing in large conference centres was not helping my poor old spine, which had certainly taken a battering over the years. In many ways I regretted giving up the original school which Tony and I had started together, and getting involved in such an uncaring commercial concern.

What I really wanted was my own school. The British School of Reflexology – that was what I would call it.

My next most dominant ambition was to have a healing centre of my own. I envisaged a lovely building in a beautiful setting where small groups of students could be professionally trained in a perfect environment and I could teach things 'my way' and not be under someone else's control. The same old problem was rearing its head once more: I was being restrained and controlled by an individual in America who was dictating exactly what I could and could not do. I was acting out somebody else's role.

So I gave myself a good talking-to again, just as I had done when I was in a hopeless mental and physical state during the breakdown of my marriage. 'If you are sure you can write books, develop a new school, why are you letting somebody else pull the strings? Alternatively you are going to be working for somebody else for the rest of your working life, getting more and more frustrated and resentful as the years go by.'

I really longed to do things 'my way'. I had repeated dreams about my own healing centre. I pictured a large room with rows of medical couches, and every time I had a dream the room was always pink and white. It had lavender-pink walls and a deep pink fitted carpet, the couches had deep pink covers and there were lots of baskets of hanging ferns. I nurtured my dream and ambition for over a year and it did not become any less vivid as the months went by. I did look around at larger houses in the area, but they were all too expensive and some were in poor condition. Then there was the recurring problem of stairs, which would mean installing a stair lift.

One morning I realised that I need not look far for my centre. I already had the ideal setting for it. My bungalow was set in a third of an acre of grounds and there was a very large space at one side in which a huge room could be built. That was it, the decision was made, I would build my dream centre and sever my contract with America, which would be difficult and cause a lot of bad feeling. It would be hard to cut the ties with my brother as we were partners in business, and I knew that my parents would think me mad to take out a mortgage twice the size of the one I already had. Logically I suppose it was a risk, particularly for someone with a considerable disability and still with dependent children, but I knew in my heart that this was right for me and if I did not do what I really wanted to do, then I would be forever wishing that I had.

I sought the advice of an architect who drew up plans which were submitted to the local council. After a lot of alteration to the plans and all the usual red tape procedures that one has to go through, the plans were passed. I then contacted several building firms for estimates and was shocked at the huge increase in building costs. The next step in the procedure was to go to the Building Society and see if I could arrange to borrow the extra money. There was then a considerable wait, which was good because first I had a special event to look forward to and plan. Clare and John were to be married in the old church at Hatfield Heath, the church they went to as children, the church where Heather was christened, and where all the festive occasions organised by the local school were held. Clare had sung in the church when she was nine or ten, and remembered being paid 50p for singing at weddings and 25p for funeral services!

We acquired a new addition to our family that year, an adorable puppy. The last and smallest of a litter of eight, Bonnie was a cross between a boxer and a labrador and really a most handsome-looking animal with a bronze coat and a soft black velvet muzzle. When Heather brought her to see me, holding this little five-week-old scrap over her shoulder, there was never any doubt that she was here to stay.

Bonnie proved to be a most amenable animal, so placid and affectionate, and soon responded to command. Her only rather destructive activity was to chew off all our indoor plants at the base, and so we had a large selection of pots full of earth, housing just one inch of a stump. She carried out these games during the night, but apart from that she destroyed nothing else, so we got off lightly.

My early love for animals was still as strong as ever, and Bonnie brought us all, especially me, hours of pleasure and company. She was forever by my side, would sit in the car for hours looking out of the window and surveying all around her, and although so docile and placid by nature, she was a superb guard dog and would create a lot of noise if anybody came near the house, so she gave us all a sense of security as we knew we were safe from any intrusion with Bonnie around. Her favourite treat was oranges and she would drool at the mouth if ever anyone peeled one. My family told me that when I was away on my trips she would lie inside the front door watching anxiously for any car that came up the drive and become quite depressed until I returned.

Although we had had a dog as children and I later inherited an adult dog from friends of mine who emigrated, Bonnie was special. She was so highly intelligent and gentle and I cannot express how much pleasure she brings.

John's 'little Princess' was married on 19 July 1986. She really did look like a princess with her true natural beauty, naturally curly long fair hair, flawless complexion and perfect features. She wore an off-the-shoulder white dress with a hooped skirt, flowers in her hair and carried a parasol. Her husband wore morning dress, as did his brothers and father. I felt very proud as my father gave her away, still youthful though in his mid-seventies and looking extremely smart in his top hat and tails. It was a wonderful day, warm and sunny, and the service, the reception, the good wishes, meeting so many friends and relations again made it a perfect day in every way. My only sadness was for her father who had missed so much by not being able to survive long enough to see his children grow up.

I organised their reception in a local hotel. We had 80 guests for dinner in the afternoon and then an evening buffet for all their young friends.

Clare and John bought a very nice house only two miles away from us, so we saw them frequently. In fact there always seems to be somebody popping in to our house. The few odd hours I get on my own are precious and I usually take advantage of the solitude to get on with writing – Bonnie always sits on my feet when I begin typing so I have a permanent 'foot muff'.

I started writing my book and thoroughly enjoyed putting every chapter together. I put in as much time as I possibly could, but seemed to be able to manage a chapter a month. This was achieved by spending at least half of every Sunday, when I was not teaching at classes, and perhaps one evening a week on it. My son Jonathan said he would design the front cover and would also do all the medical anatomical drawings, which saved a lot of money, and my little book *Reflexology: The Ancient Answer to Modern Ailments* soon became ready in draft form.

Jonathan at this time had gained entrance to the British School of Osteopathy, where he was to complete a four-year course which would eventually qualify him as a doctor of osteopathy.

Building work on my healing centre started in September 1986. As we were surrounded by so many large trees, and deep roots from the remnants of old trees, the extension had to be built on 'pilings'. This meant a very big job with a lot of heavy machinery in and out of my lovely front garden. However, there was nothing that could be done about it except to put up with the mud, mess and muddle and just keep on visualising how wonderful it would be by Christmas. The builders had said that it would take about four months to complete. From the muddy depths of the foundations came walls, then two very large windows, one at each end of the building, and a large sliding door which would open out on to a patio and fish pond. By then my garden was just like a muddy lake with deep indentations from the wheels of heavy lorries, a concrete mixer, and lots of heavy feet going backwards and forwards, digging and delving. It was going up faster than I imagined. At the end of each week when the builders had gone home for the week-end I used to go out into the extension and count the rows of bricks laid that week. The roof went on in November, and then the plasterers moved in. The area looked enormous to me: in fact it was 36' × 15'. Finally the glaziers put glass in the windows, the electrician fitted 16 ceiling lights and then we had industrial dryers in to try to dry out the room so that we could start decorating and furnishing.

In December the decorators arrived. This was the best part because now I could add colours and create the atmosphere that would be an expression of myself. Of course, just as my dreams had predicted, I chose lavender-pink with plaster panelling on the walls, and on the inside of the framework of the panelling I chose plaques, one of a lady in long flowing robes carrying a water urn and the other of a lady carrying a basket of fruit.

Deep pink fitted carpet arrived, pink and grey blinds and then the massage couches and chairs covered in silver grey dralon. Pine bookshelves lined two walls, and I bought a hi-fi system so that just the right kind of relaxing music could be played. With windows at both ends the view wherever you looked out was of conifers, shrubs, roses and a large selection of fruit trees in the back garden. It really was a healing sanctuary.

Why I did not have sleepless nights when I added up the large mortgage I had taken on, plus the huge expenses for furnishing and equipping my centre, I do not know, but in fact I never once had a single qualm that what I intended to do would not be successful. It would be the realisation of all my dreams.

21 Fulfilment

My Healing Centre was complete; in fact it was more beautiful even than I had imagined. I added little finishing touches, wicker baskets with hanging plants – I even found a pink and grey trailing plant!

I started some extra private courses for students already in training who wanted extra individual attention. We started off with just four or five students which was so successful that within six months we had twelve attending. Everybody enjoyed the individual attention that I was able to give and found the atmosphere, as they said, 'very relaxing and full of healing vibes'! We added superb wholefood and vegetarian lunches to our service – I employed a lady to help with this.

At this time Joyce, who had helped me in the house for 15 years, retired. I was sad to see her go although I could see that she had become very tired and had had enough of other people's housework. She had enough to do coping with her own home and beloved animals.

Mary, who took her place, was the wife of one of my patients. Tom had been coming to me for a long time as he suffered frequently from kidney stones and Reflexology seemed to be the only treatment that ever gave him relief. Mary proved to be an excellent housekeeper, taking on just about anything and everything, including taking Bonnie for a walk, doing any sewing jobs that I ignored, and catering for the students at the courses. She took a lot of trouble and pride in everything she did and thereby removed an enormous burden from my shoulders.

Deciding to publish my book myself, I sought out a small local specialised publishing company. I left my manuscript and drawings and they were turned like magic into a really professional, smart little book with an attractive coloured cover, beige and ochre, depicting the Egyptians working upon each other's feet, sitting on the sand with the pyramids in the background. My little book seemed to go through so many procedures before it actually became a book – in fact it took a year to put together. Eventually the first 2000 were delivered in January 1987. When I saw 2000 copies unloaded from the van I could not imagine how they could possibly all be sold. The volume of books completely filled the floor area of a small office and stood about four feet high, and when I saw the quantity I began to wonder if I had made a great mistake in taking on the responsibility of publishing it myself. Perhaps I should have left the job to Thorsons, who were quite prepared to do the job for me.

However, it did not seem long before the first 100 copies were sold and then more and more people seemed to order a copy and before long I was serving quite a large number of bookshops and so the huge mountain, or so it seemed to be, became smaller and smaller.

In January 1987 I went on my last trip to Switzerland. I would certainly miss the lovely people whom I had met over those interesting years, but I was so excited at the prospect of developing my own school that the pain of parting from my contacts in Switzerland was not quite so acute.

My book was selling well and I was now working on developing my own chart of the feet showing the areas in the feet that mirrored the internal working of the body. If you have your own school, then you have to produce your own findings of the relationship of the body to the feet. I wanted to use the words 'British School of Reflexology'. As yet, there was no such school, and to form a professional school with a strong foundation and rigid standard of training was my aim. Everything about my school was going to be of 'best quality' from the standard of training, which was of paramount importance, to the quality of the covers on the medical massage couches – pink ones, of course.

I applied to the Secretary of State for permission and was quite surprised at the rules and regulations attached to using the word 'British'. References had to be obtained from as many 'medical bodies' as possible, and so I approached various medical associations who were aware of my work in the field of alternative medicine, and various charitable organisations that I had worked for offered their services in promoting my desire to form a British Association. It did take several months, nine in fact, before a large official certificate from the Secretary of State for England and Wales arrived one morning, giving me permission to form the British School of Reflexology. Hallelujah, I had done it.

I am a great believer in presentation, so decided on a large glossy brochure advertising the training course offered and showing my own holistic healing centre. I employed a local artist to draw the centre set beautifully in its lovely gardens with my cherubic water fountain and fish pond, pink water lilies as well. This artist friend of mine did an excellent job. From these drawings a glossy pink and white brochure was produced. It was very attractively designed and the wording inside created, I hope, the impression of a training establishment with a holistic, harmonious approach, a caring attitude to the needs of the student.

22 Disabilities and how to cope with them

I have purposely not swamped this book with the daily frustrations and problems that arise when one has a physical disability, because it would make too heavy reading. In any case I have learnt to cope with most things that confront me, even if in a rather clumsy haphazard way. Disability brings difficulties round every corner, but as I have limped along for 40 years now, in a way it is probably compensatory in that I know little else. Although it must be wonderful to wear high-heeled shoes, to be able to run up a flight of stairs and to be able to command your body to do whatever you want it to do, it is possible to live a full life without these benefits, provided you put your brain into the right gear and don't feel sorry for yourself.

The main problem with disability is that it is always with you. You never have a day off. Every day of your life brings challenges, stresses, something else to try to cope with. Flights of stairs are a hurdle, and without a handrail are impossible, uneven pavements cause falls when you have to walk with a stiff leg. A shopping bag and a walking stick are quite awkward to handle, especially when the shopping bag becomes full and you realise you have bought more goods than you can carry! Slippery pavements in winter are a nightmare, and strong winds which make you feel even more unsteady than ever.

In your own environment when accessibility to most things can be organised to suit your needs, it is reasonably easy to cope, but problems arise when you go away on holiday and accommodation and facilities are not as convenient as the ones you left at home. You feel rather like a snail out of its shell. I used to find it much easier to walk about when I had prams to push – but you can't keep on having babies just to aid your walking!

When I was a teenager, I fought against any help, hoping to prove to the world that I could cope with all this alone and I did. However, as you get older you get tired of coping with it and learn to accept help offered graciously. Now as I approach 50 I have begun to ask for help wherever I can get it, and most people I find are only too happy to assist. I do use the disabled section in supermarkets and get the assistants to pack my bags. I do use the disabled parking facilities and really appreciate my orange badge – in fact I get very annoyed when I see fit, able-bodied people taking up the limited parking spaces for the disabled.

After driving round our town the other week for over half an hour trying to find a parking space, I decided to park right behind a large Renault which did not have a badge and was taking up a 'disabled' parking space. I parked as close to his bumper as I could get and went into the supermarket. I knew exactly what would happen when I came out and was ready to have a word with the owner of the Renault. Sure enough, half an hour later I came out of the supermarket to find the owner of the Renault, red in the face with rage, strumming his fingers on the bonnet of his car. I decided to use some very subtle psychology this time, and so, looking the offender directly in the eyes, I said, 'Don't you think you are bloody selfish, a fit young man like you? Have you any idea of the problems that you cause to people like me? If you want me to move my car away from the back of yours, I will give you the job of loading all this shopping into my boot, the alternative is that I shall remain with my car at the back of yours.'

He coughed and spluttered and looked terribly embarrassed, the red face turning deadly white. 'Well, you see, I was in a hurry,' was his reply. 'You are lucky to be able to hurry,' I said. 'I never can.' Very sheepishly he did load all my huge supplies of groceries very neatly into the boot of my car, asked if I would like him to lock the boot for me, which he did. I gave him a beaming smile, moved my car away from the back of his and he actually waved me goodbye, so peace was restored and I rather think he might have learnt a good lesson.

Circulation is always a great problem with polio cases, although as I don't go out walking long distances I don't get subjected to extremes of temperature. When I was young and obviously not able to drive and had to get to school or college I remember occasions when my leg became so frozen that I could actually stick a needle into it without feeling any pain. When heat comes back into the limb there is real intense pain once again. I am afraid the thermostat does not work when there is no muscle tone.

Getting out of a bath is difficult, so I stick to a shower. I live in a beautiful bungalow with just one step up to the front door and one step down to the back. Harlow is luckily a very flat town so that helps, no steep hills to climb, it is all a matter of adaptation. I can, however, walk quite long distances if I can hold on to someone's arm.

I would say that I have found a very special inner peace. I am a contented, satisfied individual, with no further strong ambitions to realise, apart from finishing and publishing this book and continuing my work in the field of alternative medicine until I am too old to do it any longer. There is pleasure to be gained in seeing tense, anxious patients come to me in considerable pain and just a few days later to see the joy and amazement on their faces that Reflexology, which is a comparatively simple science, can bring so much relief.

I see so much beauty in life to which many others seem blind, and then there is my great joy in enjoying a wide range of music. My frequent trips to the swimming pool are one of my greatest pleasures. There is no disability in water, so you can escape from it even if for only an hour or so. In water you can jump, walk, swim at speed and do everything else that others can do. Perhaps in the next life I will return as a dolphin.

Many people have remarked on my general exuberance for life and positive mental attitude. 'What is your secret?' they ask. 'What are your religious beliefs?' Religion has nothing whatsoever to do with being positive or exuberant. I do firmly believe that there is an infinite power flowing through life, an indestructible, indefinable life-force. These forces are on different levels. We may, through force of circumstances, sink to the bottom of the pit and latch on to a weak, frail, life-force characterised by negative attitudes, the 'if onlys', and 'I might have done this' and 'I nearly did that' – a life full of ifs and buts, the negative approach to everything and everybody, blaming life for all our failures and for all our problems. At this level we might just as well 'join forces with the devil' and give up altogether!

Or we can choose a more positive level of life when we confront life's knocks with courage and face up to problems, knowing and believing that all will turn out well in the end. When you believe that everything will turn out well, somehow it usually does. Eventually, if you try, you can work your way up through these levels of life, until each day begins to be a happy, fulfilling experience, there are few disaster areas now and you will lose fear. Fear is at the root of most things and is totally destructive. If we are constantly frightened of losing our job, or of developing some dreaded disease, and spend most of our waking hours worrying about worry, which only attracts back more worry, we won't make much headway. It is rather like being afraid of a barking dog. If he senses your fear he will bark even louder. If you throw a boomerang into a field it will return to you and sometimes, if you throw with accuracy, it will land almost at your feet. If you give out love, joy, compassion, these qualities will be returned to you in abundance. As within, so without: cause and effect.

If you feel sad and lonely, it is your own choice that you are as you feel. There must be somebody living very near to you who is also lonely – what about taking the first step to arrange a get-together?

Indecision is another very negative, destructive emotion. If you really feel you wish to achieve or do something different with your life, then go right ahead and 'have a go', regardless of whatever anybody else feels about your decision. It will not work if you go in with a mass of doubts, you must commit yourself 100 per cent, whether you want to paint a picture, start your own business or go back to evening school to study a subject that has interested you for many years.

I do not feel the need, therefore, to enter a church to be in tune with my creator, because I feel at one within myself and can offer out all the positive, loving, warm thoughts to others by standing, if I so wish, in the middle of a garden. In fact, I am far more in tune with life in those situations than I ever am within the confines of a church.

Heaven and hell are here on earth, and we enter into the kingdom of both several times in our lives.

It is always confusing to accept the Christian view of going to church to 'pray for the peace of the world'. It is pointless praying for the peace of the world, man has first to make peace within his own heart and within his own home, and have good relationships with his neighbours. When he has conquered and got this right he will 'infect' each and every person he meets with his goodwill, and then there might be a chance of restoring peace in the world.

Christianity should be a 'doing' not a 'praying' commitment. It is of far more use to mankind if I befriend a lonely patient in hospital or visit someone who is dying in a hospice, as I do, than go into a church and pray for him or her.

I am sure that there are a lot of very good Christians who are committed to the church, but equally there are many wonderful Christians outside it. I remember a certain situation that arose when I became involved in some church activities when my children were younger and attending Sunday School. I went to help with some flower arrangements for the harvest festival and was quite appalled at the jealousies and petty squabbling that arose over who was going to use which vase, the arguments and bad feeling about which vase should stand in which place in the church, and even more tension on which flowers each were to use. This episode ended with four very red-faced ladies who had worked themselves up over absolutely nothing who were very regular churchgoers, as were all their families, yet who caused such unrest over 'flower arrangements'. I left them to their own personal war, satisfying myself that it did not need five women to arrange flowers in one small church in any case.

I do know that when you find this 'inner peace', this warm glow of satisfaction, you do not become sick, which proves undoubtedly that tension and unhappiness cause illness. I used to be forever ailing, particularly in my years as a frustrated teenager; bronchitis, asthma, sinus trouble, skin eruptions – you name it, I had it. Those conditions were the result of my inner turmoil. Then again, during the unhappy period of my marriage, I endured more eczema and illness. During these long years that I have spent on my own with the responsibility of my family, I have been freed from emotional tension, and even though I have taken on the most enormous financial commitments in realising my dream, my health has been excellent – in fact, I have had only three days' sickness in 11 years.

Conclusion

By January 1989, my school had developed beyond my wildest dreams, and I now had another venue in Hinckley, Leicestershire. In the summer I was to go back to my beloved Switzerland to teach Reflexology at the Nurse Training School in Geneva. My ambition was now to open another school in Glasgow; I felt drawn to the area and felt it would be right for me to take Reflexology there. There seemed to be plenty of interest but no real professional training body.

The children were all thriving. Mark was doing well in his career in the field of chemistry, and was now in charge of quite a large department. Jonathan was in his third year of study in osteopathy, and I had no doubt that he would be highly successful in his chosen career.

Heather at 17 had her heart set on a career in nursing, which she is cut out for. She has good relationships with people of all ages, and when asked at the college for her second choice of career, replied that there was really nothing else she wanted to do. So maybe it is she who will be a second Florence Nightingale.

Clare gave birth to a son, James, in May – so I was now a granny, but as that made me feel really old I decided to be called 'Granann'.

My dog Bonnie had produced ten adorable puppies the previous September – had I the health and strength, I would have kept at least four of them!

My home and garden are very important to me, primarily because our home has a very special atmosphere, which many have remarked upon. I have no desire for gold or diamonds or a big fast car, but if I could have one extravagant wish it would be for a large, heated, indoor swimming pool with a magnificent stereo unit – the speakers set into the walls – in which I could swim every day to a background of my favourite music. One day, maybe.

I shall continue to increase my knowledge, continue to reaffirm my faith in myself, and every night give blessings to all the wonderful people who have worked with me throughout my career.

When at night I close the curtains on another day and maybe look up to a star on a cloudless night, I remember when I was a small child being told by a special aunt that stars were the true spirits of those who had died and passed on to another world, and that those true spirits looked down on the loved ones that they had been separated from and watched over and protected them. Although that is only a childhood story, it is somehow a comforting expression of the life hereafter. If John does have any contact with us all here on earth I can only say to him, 'I do love you – I made some stupid mistakes but everything I did was in defence of our children.'

Knowledge is like love; the more you give out the more you get back.